In Hora Mortis ✝ Under the Iron of the Moon

The Lockert Library of Poetry in Translation
Editorial Advisor: Richard Howard
For other titles in the
Lockert Library
see page 167

‡

In Hora Mortis ✣ Under the Iron of the Moon

Poems by Thomas Bernhard

Translated by James Reidel

PRINCETON UNIVERSITY PRESS ✣ PRINCETON AND OXFORD

Published by Princeton University Press, 41 William Street, Princeton,
New Jersey 08540
In the United Kingdom: Princeton University Press, 3 Market Place,
Woodstock, Oxfordshire OX20 1SY

In Hora mortis, first published 1958, Otto Müller Verlag, Salzburg
© 1991 Suhrkamp Verlag, Frankfurt am Main
Unter dem Eisen des Mondes, first published 1958, Kiepenheuer & Witsch,
Köln © 1991 Suhrkamp Verlag, Frankfurt am Main

Grateful acknowledgment is given to *WebConjunctions*,
where this translation of *In Hora Mortis* first appeared, and *Artful Dodge*
for "The year is like a year a thousand years ago."

Library of Congress Cataloging-in-Publication Data

Bernhard, Thomas.
[In hora mortis. English]
In hora mortis ; Under the iron of the moon : poems / by Thomas
Bernhard; translated by James Reidel.
p. cm.—(The Lockert library of poetry in translation)
Includes index.
ISBN-13: 978-0-691-12641-8 (cloth : alk. paper)
ISBN-10: 0-691-12641-0 (cloth : alk. paper)
ISBN-13: 978-0-691-12642-5 (pbk. : alk. paper)
ISBN-10: 0-691-12642-9 (pbk. : alk. paper)
I. Title: In hora mortis ; Under the iron of the moon.   II. Reidel,
James.   III. Bernhard, Thomas. Unter dem Eisen des Mondes.
English.   IV. Title: Under the iron of the moon.   V. Title.
VI. Series.

PT2662.E715 2006
833'.914—dc22   2005054534

British Library Cataloging-in-Publication Data is available

This book has been composed in Aldus Roman

Printed on acid-free paper ∞

pup.princeton.edu

Printed in the United States of America

1 3 5 7 9 10 8 6 4 2

The Lockert Library of Poetry in Translation is supported by a bequest
from Charles Lacy Lockert (1888–1974).

Contents

Translator's Preface

I speak the language that I alone understand, no one else, the same
as anybody understands only his own language;
and the ones who think they understand
are blockheads and
charlatans.

—Thomas Bernhard*

Dichter, the German word for poet, is often an honorific title.
It can be given to a writer who has written nothing but prose
and no verse at all. This is the case for the Austrian novelist
and playwright Thomas Bernhard (1931–1989), whose legacy
as a poet is little known—and even economically omitted
from some chronologies and biographical entries—though he
himself never let go of this role. This volume presents the sec-
ond and third books of Bernhard's poetry, which appeared in
the late 1950s and before he reinvented himself and his career
with his first major prose works.

Such reinventions usually spring from failure and frus-
tration. Bernhard, however, soon after graduating from Salz-
burg's Mozarteum in 1957, published his first collection, *Auf
der Erde und in der Hölle* (*On Earth and in Hell*). The great
playwright and literary critic Carl Zuckmayer wrote effu-

---

* From a speech given in Vienna, 1968.

sively about the debut of this young lyric poet, who wore his hair like a London teddy boy or the late James Dean and took up where Georg Trakl and expressionism left off two world wars ago:

> These poems are, perhaps, a discovery greater than any I have ever made during the last decade in our literature . . . they have the distinguishing features of great modern poetry.

Bernhard worked intensively and almost exclusively on his poetry throughout the 1950s. If he and his poems were seen as a leitmotif, they would stand in contrast to his later novels with their aging, unresolved alter egos and their unfinished and even unstarted grand projects. In one respect, however, there is a resemblance: being the young poet was almost a hermetic performance for Bernhard, and the verse itself was deeply personal in subject matter. Nevertheless, he intended to win for himself a reputation with his work. The leading avant-garde journals published his poems, including *Stimmen der Gegenwart* (*Contemporary Voices*), which featured the work of many of Vienna's young postwar, post-occupation literati. And, while studying theater at the Mozarteum, Bernhard gave rare public readings. It was no secret that he aspired to be an important poet, and his shyness and reclusivity seemed as much designed for the posturing and persona of a very serious and very Austrian *poète maudit* who would, at the right time, segue to the position of a laureate. That is, he wanted to make a name for himself in what had become a renaissance in contemporary German verse and in one of its epicenters. In some of Bernhard's poems, the word *Ruhm*, which means fame, the glory from success, seems premeditated as well as abhorred.

Ingeborg Bachmann, a fellow Austrian, served as his example to follow. She had already garnered considerable recognition with her first two books of poetry and her radio plays.

Her early-won fame, too, had more than the obvious dimension that made it attractive (her appearance on the cover of *Der Spiegel* in 1955). She also had a *style* for keeping a distance between herself and Austria, a stage that certainly needed its male lead, too, which Bernhard could supply. This might explain where his energy came from, despite ill health from the tuberculosis he contracted as an adolescent, to write three cycles of poetry and to prepare himself in every way for the role of a public poet. Ingrid Bülau, the concert pianist, who studied with Bernhard at the Mozarteum, saw this in her shy, pockmarked friend when she invited him to her parents' home in Hamburg during their vacations from school. There he would tape himself on the family's reel-to-reel recorder, reciting his poems over and over, erasing and rerecording them in order to get his reading voice right, with the correct modulations, timbres, and pauses all in place—as if he were trying to play a musical composition like his beloved Glenn Gould—foreshadowing the obsessed artists of his fiction. The sisterly young woman's presence at these private readings especially points to that pathological performance-narcissism found in *The Lime Works,* in which Bernhard the poet returns as the frustrated writer Konrad, who recites sentences hundreds of times slowly and then hundreds of times rapidly to his invalid wife—whose brains he will blow out as if to show what he has done by *reading* them into the consistency of "Emmenthaler cheese."

Otto Müller Verlag brought out Bernhard's first book, *On Earth and in Hell,* for the very reason that he was its voice *in extremis* in what had become a literary exploration into *Herkunfskomplex.* This deliberately Freudian-like term describes the young German-language writer's problematic relationship with origin, with roots, the soil, family, and home. That language has a word for all these things, *Heimat.* For Bernhard and his contemporaries in Upper Austria, Carinthia, and the rest of the Hapsburg heartland, this meant finding and self-accepting one's rural origins vis-à-vis the very recent Nazi past and its literature. This meant not so much dealing with the anxiety of influence but rather with the anxiety of the very landscape and what happened in it and what was buried beneath it. The novels and poetry of National Socialism celebrated the ancient and purifying Germanic soil so as to counter the decadent Jewish and Bolshevik cosmopolitanism of modernism. Bernhard's poems and the poems of Bachmann, Paul Celan, and others were composed under and very much against this powerful shadow—but in Bernhard one also finds a peculiarly painful and autobiographical dimension. He was the illegitimate son of a kind of Austrian grifter and the out-of-wedlock daughter of Johannes Freumbichler, a ne'er-do-well and late-blooming writer who became a role model for his grandson. The mother, Herta Fabjan—her surname evincing her mother's marriage to another man at the time of her birth—had died young, in 1950, and her memory, as well as the malevolence of Nazism, illuminates the first poems:

> In my mother's garden,
> my rake gathers the stars
> that fell while I was gone.
> The night is warm and my limbs
> radiate their green descent,
> flowers and leaves,
> the blackbird's call and the loom's clatter.
> In my mother's garden,
> I stamp barefoot on the snakeheads
> that peer through the rusty gate
> with flaming tongues.

In 1958 Otto Müller and Kiepenheuer & Witsch, a trade house in Cologne, published Bernhard's next two books respectively, *In Hora Mortis* and *Unter dem Eisen des Mondes* (*Under the Iron of the Moon*). These collections could also be called *Heimat* poems. However, the first is an address to the God found in that landscape—the other to its existential cemetery and its *purgatorio*. Here Bernhard found Austrian soil—and its air, fire, and water as well—to be like a hair shirt and a blanket. It is a killing ground but with a postcard setting to soften the blows, the perfect vantage to apprehend "the peace which passeth understanding." Both books show how much Bernhard had read outside German-language literature, that he had T. S. Eliot in mind and particularly Eliot's religious poems—the ones that alienated that post-*Waste Land* generation of poets who bought into Eliot's nihilism. Indeed Bernhard, whose novels and theater were setups (*vide* the scandal of his novel *Woodcutters*), may have learned his craft for this in part from carnivalizing "Ash Wednesday" along with the rest of the Jazz Age poet's dandyish Anglo-Catholic tap-dancing and with a better ear for the French Symbolists. The young Bernhard actually reads like someone *burned* by faith—which I see both ways—and giving more than a "penny for the Old Guy." (Bernhard would give his nod to Eliot later, with an epigraph from *The Waste Land* beginning his cycle *Ave Vergil*.)

But is it carnival? The young Bernhard can sound deathly serious when he writes, "Your voice will be my voice / in bitterness." It sounds like no empty threat, given his later achievements and acerbic reputation. It's as if he is both awed and appalled by the horrific, godlike powers and role that he is taking on as a young writer, unavoidably full of himself like a disease, that pierce through him with as much pain as the chest punctures he received as a TB patient (a near-death experience that echoes so much here). If one were looking for a teleology, could it be in this lyric? Where did that avenging angel, sitting in judgment, "sitting in the wing chair" and thinking his *Woodcutters* thoughts, stage his purpose? Then there is the mystical religiosity. *In Hora Mortis* consists of prayer-like verses spoken by a tormented "believer." These sound so personal, so visceral, as to seem more genuine, more alone, than Eliot's grand faith, which was so public and reiterated as to suggest that he was really a newer doubting

Translator's Preface

⊷ ⊷

xi

Thomas, that he even faked it. If Bernhard's is a performance piece, which I think it is, one only has to see its unavoidable histrionics, whether recited inside the reader's head or, if one dares, read aloud. No other rationalization is needed—but there are other ways to see that "something else is going on."

As the Beats and other liberating poets and movements made inroads into Cold War Europe, Bernhard was also confronted by the new fashions and the strong revival in German-language poetry, which included its postwar redis-covery in England and the United States—where City Lights and New Directions published anthologies of young German poets. (The latter included Bernhard.) Nevertheless, his poems seemed to be a throwback, a kind of Austrian mimesis of Baudelaire, Rimbaud, and Verlaine. In hindsight, however, they are far more modern and relevant now than the shop-worn experimental writing of that era. There is an alternative to the nuclear angst of the 1950s that we have back again in our own time, which is but a subcategory, next to the Freudian one—these poems take on the *ur*-Angst itself, the fear of death, of meaninglessness, of extinction. Only the sheer con-ceit of Bernhard's plaint for "God" to hear can clue us to the comedy, that it might be better to get it all over with, that any more of our religio-hermetic torture is absurd, a tasteless performance. Another poet-novelist from Bernhard's part of the world, Franz Werfel, in the context of the approaching Holocaust, also addressed God in his expressionist verse; but Werfel, with his "world friend" persona, has this Jewish-Catholic awe whereas Bernhard is this pietà-form shivering in God and Austria's lap, stealing the show from all others. His poems are palinodic, a verse of retraction, of growth and rot in the same breath for the Austrian Eden, of the consola-tion and disconsolation of an Austrian Catholic death in which Bernhard is its culture-victim and reenactor. God is given His due, but it is such bad acting, such an overfeeding of passion and *self*-extreme unction handed back as an enor-mous ethical farce. (What Bernhard does to the divine audience points to what he did to the human audiences of his fiction and theater.) In *In Hora Mortis*, the cosmic joke is especially played on *that* hour's divine Author and this impression is right there, where it would seem to be missed, in Bernhard's "real" and *faux* pietism and that teary-eyed and eternal—and not necessarily Germanic—weakness for *Klagerei*, the undulant moaning about pains and wrongs to some higher authority. It is a send-up and critique of the tragic sense of life even as one ascribes to it. The long-winded plaintive cry is really Bernhard philosophically *exhausting* Unamuno.

There is more to the *Iberian* flavor of these poems (Spain is where they resonated first in translation), and it is not comedy or carnival. The Catalan translator of *In Hora Mortis* added to the title *Nou Salms*. In his Bernhard blog, a reader of the Spanish editions of *In Hora Mortis* and *Under the Iron of the Moon* sees a poet who "has not renounced the search for God and the preservation of his faith," even as "solitude, disgust, and the fear of death pervade everything." Bernhard passes for a pilgrim on the *Camino de Santiago*, "confronted by nature that has no hope of salvation, that has no need of it, that is radically disintegrated and decayed." He exists in a "[religious] mystery" and as one who travels along the "roads of a tormented mystic, perhaps already in an impossible crisis." In other words, Bernhard writes like a Catholic poet—or he parodies one so closely as to make it impossible to tell them apart, with a kind of method acting—and it is intriguing, despite his hair-pulling over the *criminal* damage inflicted on Austrian culture by its church, its clerics, to wonder if the role subsumed him. (He was once intrigued by the idea of being called Pope Thomas.) As the same blogger suggests, taking the poems into consideration certainly will "reorder" the received knowledge we have about this writer and his work. It will certainly cast in a new light what he does *mean*, which has always been a problem. Perhaps he had his poems and their struggle in mind during his infamous *Mallorca Monologues*. In a Spanish setting, which he always found comfortable and disarming, to an interviewer and audience who bought into his anti-Catholicism, who would think he was pulling their leg, Bernhard said he believed in a holy-card, chromo-kitsch heaven and not hell for him—that he was, in a sense, *saved*:

> I always believed in heaven, even as a child. The older I get, the more I believe in it, because heaven is something quite beautiful. In heaven they always wear freshly cleaned, white clothes. . . . And you will certainly be an angel in that heaven. I'll be flying toward you in a white shirt with pretty embroidery.

Under the Iron of the Moon is also a cycle of untitled lyrics that uses the incantatory method of *In Hora Mortis*. They continue the themes Bernhard introduced in his first book of poems, with the elegiac taken to the same undulating extremes and exaggerations as the religiosity of the sequence they follow in this volume. And they, too, seem a throwback: *Under the Iron of the Moon* could have been written by Georg Trakl—one of the Vienna Group's revered models—or Christine Lavant, an Austrian of the generation just before Bernhard's, whose influence is unmistakable to the point that Bernhard, in that delicate ecology of fame in poetry, may have ceded his poet's role for the very reason that he could offer only so much that was new and original. (As testimony of his admiration for her, he edited a selection of Lavant's best work in 1987, just before preparing his own poetry for posterity.) Or it is, in its intensification of these poets, another send-up, of overacting them, especially the hallowed Trakl.

Nevertheless, in this second act of "reconciliation" with his rural origins, Bernhard expresses wonder as well as the estrangement and disappointment that he endured when he placed himself in such a starting point, such "in-country." Here he is like a child exposed to die outside the city walls by its mother. The "exterior shots" and "outdoor performances" that would practically disappear from the novels and plays to come are present in the poems, and we can see why, perhaps, they disappear. Even with the rural serenities that Bernhard's verse is capable of, even the sound of milking ultimately has the catharsis of bathing a talking corpse in an acid bath. As Eric Ormsby notes, these poems, in which Bernhard professes his curious love–hate relationship with nature and the Austrian countryside, are also the test bed for that "stubborn earthiness" of his novel writing and "his flair for pungent invective."

To place these two books in Bernhard's canon in translation and to say as much as I have—and to have found the enthusiasm with which to endeavor for many years to see it through—still seems incongruous. Indeed, what little there was about them would seem to warn one away. Thomas Cousineau, writing in the *Review of Contemporary Fiction*, found the "decidedly religious and mystical inspiration" of some of the poems to be a curiosity for a writer who achieved his literary fame for novels and plays that are more a provocative exposé of the pathologies of his native Austria (one of these being Catholicism). The Bernhard biographer Gitta Honegger, whose focus is his theater, on which she is acute, has only chronological facts about his poetry. She even suggests a body of work that is not there, saying that Bernhard had only a "flirtation" with the concrete poetry of the colorful Vienna Group. Others called it a *Sackgasse*, a dead-end. M. A. Orthofer, in an appreciation of *Ave Vergil*, still writes that the "poems remain an aside" so as not to detract from the greatness of Bernhard's novels and plays. But this is followed with the observation that "Poetry came first. . . . Bernhard was a poet, first."

Such mystification (or sidestepping?) would suggest that Bernhard had made a *falsche Bewegung*, a wrong move in his early years. Indeed, the great cultural noise made by a now-international industry of scholarship and hagiography that rose after his death in 1988 is muffled in regard to his poems (with exceptions here and there, such as an exhaustive thesis on the poetry's death symbols by the South Korean Tschae-Bong Noh). They do not *ruin the view* for his metromanic fictions and inflammatory stage triumphs like *Heldenplatz*. These are the course correction for the verse; but despite their excellence and Austrian state prizes, they are possibly a byproduct of wounded pride over the rejection of a book of poems. That is, given Bernhard's obsession with the failed artist–writer–scholar–actor, the stuff of his success could be intensely shoveled dirt on what was Bernhard the *Lyriker*. The literary pranking on his homeland may be far more personal and enormous than we know.

For his part, Bernhard did not consider his poetry a pariah; he even returned to it. *Ave Vergil*, though written in England in 1960, was published in 1981. And near the end of his life, he took a keen interest in collecting his published poems and making sure that they had a prominent place in his oeuvre, his origins as a writer. Nor should one fail to see in the plays the morphological similarity to poetry on the printed page. Indeed, the way Bernhard's dramaturgy is scripted, without punctuation, probably originated in his verse-writing. *Die Irsinn, Die Häftlinge* (*The Lunatics, The Inmates*), "two" poems typographically rendered as one and published in a limited edition in 1962, requires, at the least, a private performance. One would have to read it before a mirror, the way the celebrated and dissolute Austrian actor Oskar Werner performed poetry recitals for himself during his years without work.

The reason that these two books can be presented together is that they represent Bernhard the poet at a crucial phase, when he *felt* at the height of his powers. There is a great deal of revision in his collected poems. However, these two books are, for the most part, in their original form. Bernhard's personal copy of *Unter dem Eisen des Mondes* has a note on the flyleaf that, written years later when he began to gather, revise, and edit his verse, suggests the kind of confidence and satisfaction the poems in this book held for him: "my own copy, that today—7.12.1980—pleased me very well. Thomas B." Additionally, a year before his death in 1988, he approved the republication of *In Hora Mortis* in a new chapbook edition.

Despite the three books of poetry, in 1961 an Austrian publisher rejected Bernhard's fourth, a collection of over one hundred poems that so far remains unpublished. All that remains of this ambitious cycle is its title. It stands as a kind of marker over the crushed and disappointed young poet's transfiguration into the Bernhard of official biographies and the growing shelves of critical writing about him. Bernhard gave the title to his first novel, *Frost*, which he wrote in seven weeks in 1962. Its publication soon brought him recognition among such contemporaries as Bachmann and established him as Austria's most important young novelist, a reputation he consolidated with *Amras*, published two years later. From that time Bernhard did not write poetry again. He subsequently debuted as a playwright with *Ein Fest für Boris* (*A Party for Boris*) at the end of 1970 and continued producing plays for the Burgtheater until a year before his death in 1989. With this achievement and his other novels and memoirs, his early work as a poet has practically been eclipsed.

Bernhard did not want this work to be neglected. Nearing the end of his life, he personally oversaw the editing and revision of his *Gesammelte Gedichte* (*Collected Poems*) so as to place it authoritatively with the rest of the canon. He went as far as to make it a work unto itself from which no poem could be published separately save for a few exceptions—one of which is this present collection. Here I have tried to provide an English rendering that corresponds line-by-line with the German text yet reads as naturally and *histrionically* as the original and can exist on its own. The titles, like the verse itself, have not had liberties taken with them. *In Hora Mortis* is left untranslated from the Hail Mary in its Latin original. *Unter dem Eisen des Mondes* is left as it would appear on first reading to the German eye, like the moon in the last act of Alban Berg's *Wozzeck*. However, with all the freezing in these poems, Bernhard's sky also shares something with the spiritual one described by Hölderlin (another presence in these poems) to Schiller in a letter from the summer (!) of 1794: "I freeze and stiffen in this winter that surrounds me. My sky is so iron, I am such stone." Playing in all this crisis from a title is another way to hear the word *Eisen* as the noun form of the verb *eisen* (the root *Eis* means ice), that is, to "ice," "add ice," "chill." The word is used to express that one's blood or body is turning to ice—or that one simply needs some ice in his or her drink or in a bowl of soup that is too hot. Here, then, is the possibility for a black comedy that is monstrously revelatory and speaks volumes for the writer to come. For here, if one can see it, like the proverbial moon between the trees, is this romantic image of the moon—so much stock scenery in Austro-German symbolism, like the paintings of Caspar David Friedrich, sent up as an existential lump of ice and irony.

—James Reidel

In Hora Mortis

La Luna, densa e gra[ve], densa e grave,
come sta, la luna?

•

Der Mond, dicht und schwer, dicht und schwer,
wie bleibt er [schweben}, der Mond?

•

—Leonardo Da Vinci, *Philosophische Tagebücher*

•

In Hora Mortis*

La Luna, densa e gra[ve], densa e grave,
come sta, la luna?

·

The Moon, dense and profound, dense and profound,
how does it stay [aloft], the moon?

·

—Leonardo Da Vinci, *Philosophical Diaries*

·

*The title is taken from the closing line of the Latin version of the Hail Mary, "nunc et in hora mortis nostrae" (now and at the hour of our death).
In Hora Mortis was orginally published as a chapbook
in 1958 in Salzburg by Otto Müller
Verlag. It is Bernhard's
second book.

·

I

Wild wächst die Blume meines Zorns
und jeder sieht den Dorn
der in den Himmel sticht
daß Blut aus meiner Sonne tropft
es wächst die Blume meiner Bitternis
aus diesem Gras
das meine Füße wäscht
mein Brot
o Herr
die eitle Blume
die im Rad der Nacht erstickt
die Blume meines Weizens Herr
die Blume meiner Seele
Gott verachte mich
ich bin von dieser Blume krank
die rot im Hirn mir blüht
über mein Leid.

In Hora Mortis

I

The flower of my anger grows wild
and everyone sees its thorn
piercing the sky
so that blood drips from my sun
growing the flower of my bitterness
from this grass
that washes my feet
my bread
o Lord
the vain flower
that is choked in the wheel of night
the flower of my wheat Lord
the flower of my soul
God despise me
I am sick from this flower
that blooms red in my brain
over my sorrow.

In Hora Mortis

Mein Auge quält mich Herr
und Qual macht mir mein Herz
zu einer Amsel
die nicht singt
und meine Schrift am Himmel
Gräsern fremd
o Herr mich quält der Stern
der meinen Schlaf durchschwimmt
mit Tod und Morgen reiner Seele
Herr mein Auge sieht was Dich bedrückt
und meinen Kindern Weinen treibt ins Blut
o Herr mein Auge sieht das Haus des Maurers
und den Schmerz der Welt genau
und weiß sich nicht zu helfen
wie der Baum im Winter
der mich schweigend fällt
mein Wort mein Glück mein Weinen.

In Hora Mortis

My vision torments me Lord
and torment makes my heart
into a blackbird
that does not sing
and my writing on the sky
someone else's grass
o Lord the star torments me
that floats through my sleep
with death and morning's pure soul
Lord my vision sees what depresses You
and makes my children's tears into blood
o Lord my vision sees that house of walls
and the world's pain perfectly
and doesn't know how to help itself
like the tree in winter
that silently fells me
my word my happiness my weeping.

In Hora Mortis

Ich weiß keine Straße mehr die hinaus führt
ich weiß keine Straße mehr
komm hilf
ich weiß nicht mehr
was mich befallen wird
in dieser Nacht
ich weiß nicht mehr was Morgen ist
und Abend
ich bin so allein
o Herr
und niemand trinkt mein Leiden
keiner steht an meinem Bett
und nimmt die Qual mir ab
und schickt den Wolken mich
und grünen Flüssen
die ins Meer hinrollen
Herr
mein Gott
ich bin den Vögeln ausgesetzt
dem Schlag der Uhr die berstend
meine Seele kränkt
und mir mein Fleisch verbrennt
o Herr in meinem Wort ist Finsternis
die Nacht die meine Fische schlägt
unter dem Wind
und Berge schwarzer Qual
o Herr erhöre mich
o hör mich an
ich will nicht mehr allein die Übelkeit
und diese Welt ertragen
hilf mir
ich bin tot
und wie der Apfel roll ich
in das Tal
und muß ersticken
unterm Holz des Winters

In Hora Mortis

⊷ ⚏ ⊶

6

I no longer know of a street that leads out
I no longer know of a street
come help
I don't know anymore
what will happen to me
during this night
I don't know what morning is anymore
or evening
I am so alone
o Lord
and no one partakes of my suffering
no one stands at my bed
and takes away my torment
and sends me into the clouds
and off to green rivers
that curl into the sea
Lord
my God
I am exposed to the birds
to the exploding stroke of the hour
that wounds my soul
and burns my flesh
o Lord in my word is darkness
the night that beats my fish
under the wind
and mountains of black pain
o Lord hear me
o listen to me
I don't want to be nauseated alone
and endure this world
help me
I am dead
and like an apple I roll
into the valley
and must be choked
under the log of winter

In Hora Mortis

⊷ ▨◆▨ ⊶

o mein Gott ich weiß nicht mehr
wohin mein Weg mich führt
ich weiß nicht mehr was gut und schlecht ist
auf den Feldern
Herr mein Gott in Gliedern
ich bin schwach und arm
mein Wort verbrennt in Traurigkeit
für Dich.

In Hora Mortis

o my God I don't know anymore
where my path leads
I don't know what is good and bad
in the fields
in limbs Lord my God
I am tired and poor
my word burns in grief
for You.

In Hora Mortis

Unruhe ist in den Gräsern
die Hütten sind von der Unruhe erfaßt
mich schlägt die Glocke Herr
mein Gott
wild sind die Tauben
unruhig ist auch der Mond
und seine Sichel die ins Fleisch mir stößt
Herr auch im Stall ist Unruh
und am Rand der Bäche
die den Schnee nicht fliehn
mein Gott auch Baum und Fisch
sind von der Unruhe erfaßt.

In Hora Mortis

Restlessness is in the grass
the cottages are seized by turmoil
the bell strikes me Lord
my God
the doves are wild
the moon is on edge
its sickle pierces my flesh
Lord unrest is in the sty
and at the edge of these brooks
that do not flee from the snow
my God tree and fish too
are seized by restlessness.

In Hora Mortis

II

Zerfall mein Gott
der meine Qual zu Staub stößt
vor den Tempeln
Herr mein Gott ich bin zerstört
zerschunden schon mit Kraut
und Wurzel
o zerstört mit Steinen
o zerstört im Acker
Eifersucht hat mich zerstört
in Liebe
und bespritzt mit Blut
zerstört
ich kann nicht träumen
niemand träumt
ich kann vor Dir nicht stehn
ich bin zerstört in dieser Zeit
die mir ihr Messer stößt ins Herz
o Herr der mich in Schnee und Eis läßt knien
um ein Gebet
und Gnade fernen Himmels
Herr gib Brot und Wein
und laß mich sterben jetzt
und wehn im Wind.

In Hora Mortis

II

To dust my God
who pounds my torment to dust
before the temples
Lord my God I am destroyed
already whipped to shreds with weed
and root
o destroyed by stones
o destroyed in the fields
jealousy has destroyed me
in love
and spattered with blood
destroyed
I cannot dream
no one dreams
I cannot stand before you
I am destroyed in this time
which stabs me in the heart with its knife
o Lord who lets me kneel in ice and snow
for a prayer
and Heaven's distant mercy
Lord pass bread and wine
and let me die now
and blow in the wind.

In Hora Mortis

Deine Stimme wird meine Stimme sein
in Bitternis
Deine Stimme die Sterben schüttelt
in starre Furchen
die mich zerstört
o Herr aus Nacht und Furcht stampft mein Gebet
die Sonne
und den Mond
Deine Stimme ist meine Stimme
Herr ich bin in Dir
erdrückt in meiner Qual
die zündet mir die Augen an
daß ich verbrenn mein Gott im Feuer
Deines Zorns
der seinen Stachel treibt
in mein Gehirn aus Blut.

In Hora Mortis

Your voice will be my voice
in bitterness
Your voice that shakes death
in unbending furrows
that destroys me
o Lord my prayer is pressed from night and fear
the sun
and the moon
Your voice is my voice
Lord I am in You
crushed by my torment
which sets my eyes on fire
so that I burn my God in the flames
of Your wrath
which pounds its thorn
of blood into my brain.

In Hora Mortis

Zur Rechten sitzt der Teufel
Herr der mir mein Glied zerstört
und mir das Hirn anfüllt
mit Stein und Kraut und Mühsal
langer Winter
Herr
im Fleisch das nach Dir schreit
im Staub will ich Dich suchen
Herr so richte mich
ich bin schon lang bereit
zerschlage mich mein Gott
und laß mich nicht allein
ich kann im Bett nicht ruhn
mich nimmt kein Schlaf
o Herr
vernichte mich
laß mich nicht mehr allein
nicht jetzt
in dieser Stunde
nicht im Mondverfall
und nicht mein Gott
vor Zwölf.

In Hora Mortis

To the right sits the Devil
Lord who breaks my limbs
and fills my head
with stone and cabbage and toil
in the long winter
Lord
in flesh that cries out to You
I will seek You in the dust
so Lord judge me
I have long been ready
my God destroy me
and don't leave me alone
I can't get any rest in bed
I get no sleep
o Lord
exterminate me
don't leave me alone anymore
not now
during these hours
not when the moon sinks
and not my God
before midnight.

In Hora Mortis

Ich sehe Herr was ich jetzt sehen muß
den Morgen der die Qual
nicht will und nicht mein Bett
in das es schneit
o Herr
der mein Gebet nicht will
und meine Klage frißt
im Rücken müder Sterne
reicher Äcker
finsterer Höfe
der mein Grab aufwirft
der mich erschlägt mit einem Beil
o Herr
der Mensch liebt nur
das Beil
und trinkt die Lieder nicht wie Blut
und Tod auf grünem Hügel
höher
als das Meer
o Herr
ich will was kommen muß jetzt sehn
mein Sterben Herr
und mein Vergehn in Tränen.

In Hora Mortis

I see Lord what I must see now
the morning that does not want
this torment and not my bed
in which it snows
o Lord
who does not want my prayers
and devours my cries
behind the tired stars
rich fields
dark farmhouses
who digs my grave
who chops me down with an axe
o Lord
one only loves
the axe
and doesn't drink hymns like blood
and death on green hills
higher
than the sea
o Lord
I want to see what now must come
my death Lord
and my passing away in tears.

In Hora Mortis

Wann Herr wird mein Fleisch
und dieser kalte Tod im Winter
Nacht und Mühsal
steinig und erfroren
zu den Blüten reinen Winds
die Krankheit
meiner Lieder
dieser Verse Krankheit
zu den Tropfen Taus auf grünen Hügeln
Herr
wann wird mein Sterben
frei sein näher
Deiner Seele
die mich arg betrübt?
Wann wird mein Weg
der froh begann im Schnee
aufgehn im Regen starrer Engel
Herr
im Wind mein Grab?

In Hora Mortis

When Lord will my flesh
and this cold death in this winter
night and tribulation
be petrified and frostbitten
to these flowers of sheer wind
the illness
of my songs
the sickness of these verses
to drops of dew on green hills
Lord
when will my dying
free me to be nearer
Your soul
that afflicts me so terribly?
When will my path
that began joyfully in the snow
climb into the rain of freezing angels
Lord
my grave in the wind?

In Hora Mortis

Warum fürchte ich mein Altern
meinen Tod der mich befällt
den Schrei?
Ich fürchte mich o Herr
ich fürchte meine Seele
und den Tag der an der Mauer lehnt
und mich zersägt
o Herr
ich fürchte mich
ich fürchte schon die Nacht
die vor den Dörfern steht
und hinterm Haus
die in den Kühen heult
und mit den Sternen tanzt
O Gott
ich fürchte mich
vor Dir
und vor der Traurigkeit
die mir den Mund zerschlägt
ich fürchte Herr
mein Grab
und mein Geschick in Düsternis
o Herr den Tod.

In Hora Mortis

Why do I fear my getting old
my death which afflicts me
this scream?
I fear o Lord
I fear my soul
and the day that slouches against the wall
and saws me to pieces
o Lord
I fear
I already fear the night
that is outside the villages
and behind the house
that moans in the cows
and dances with the stars
O God
I fear
before You
and before the sorrow
that smashed me in the mouth
I fear Lord
my grave
and my fate in darkness
o Lord this death.

In Hora Mortis

Der Tod ist klar im Bach
und wild im Mond
und klar
wie mir der Stern im Abend zittert
fremd vor meiner Tür
der Tod ist klar
wie Honig im August
so klar ist dieser Tod
und treu mir
wenn der Winter kommt
o Herr
schick' einen Tod mir
daß mich friert
und mir die Sprache kommt im Meer
und nah dem Feuer
Herr
der Tod fällt nachts den Baumstamm an
und mancher Amsel Schlaf
in Finsternissen.

In Hora Mortis

Death is clear in the stream
and wild in the moon
as clear
to me as the evening star that shivers
a stranger outside my door
death is clear
as honey in August
this death is so clear
and so unfailing to me
when the winter comes
o Lord
send me a death
so that I freeze
and my way to speak comes in the sea
and by the fire
Lord
each night death assails the tree
and many a blackbird's sleep
in darkness.

In Hora Mortis

III

Herr der nicht mehr lügt
o Herr
der meinen Namen spricht
und segnet meiner Lieder Schwäche
Herr
und meiner Augen Mohn
die Traurigkeit
o Herr
der mich verständigt wann
ich sterben muß
und wo
und wie
und durch der Engel Flug verstört
o schicke Herr
die Körner
wie Du sie gesät hast
zu den Armen
die vor kalten Scheunen
unterstehn
und frieren
Herr.

In Hora Mortis

III

Lord who does not lie anymore
o Lord
who speaks my name
and blesses the weakness of my songs
Lord
and the poppies of my eyes
the sorrow
o Lord
who tells me when
I must die
and where
and how
and left distraught by the angel's flight
o send Lord
the grain
the way You have sown it
to the poor
who against cold barns
take shelter
and freeze
Lord.

In Hora Mortis

Wach auf
wach auf
und höre mich
ich bin in Dir mein Gott
wach auf
und hör mich an
ich bin allein mit Dir
verbrannt zu Asche längst
und tot im Stein
der mir kein Feuer schlägt
wach auf
und hör mich an mein Gott
ich bin vor Frost schon müd
und traurig
weil mein Tag verblüht
und nicht mehr wieder kommt
was war
o Herr
mich friert
mein Schmerz ist ohne End
mein Tod kommt bald
zu mir.

In Hora Mortis

Wake up
wake up
and hear me
I am inside You my God
wake up
and listen to me
I am alone with You
long burned to ashes
and dead in the stone
that strikes no fire for me
wake up
and hear me my God
I am already tired from the frost
and sad
for my day fades
and no longer comes anymore
what was
o Lord
I freeze
my pain is without end
my death soon comes
for me.

In Hora Mortis

Wo bist Du Herr und wo
mein Glück?
Mein Trost ist hin
und meiner Augen Zahl
mein Gott
der Morgen kam und ging
in Mühsal
wo ist was ich nicht mehr bin
und wo der Schlaf
und süßer Duft der Glieder
Honig
Laub
und Wind
vom Ölberg
Herr
mein Gott
der mir den Mond beschreibt
um Mitternacht.

In Hora Mortis

Where are You Lord and where
is my happiness?
My consolation is gone
and the figure for my eyes
my God
the morning came and went
with great effort
where is what I no longer am
and where the sleep
the sweet smell of arms and legs
honey
leaves
and wind
from the Mount of Olives
Lord
my God
who describes for me the moon
at midnight.

In Hora Mortis

Die Zeit ist ausgelöscht
o Herr
mein Wort das bitter kam
und finster
Herr
zu finster für die Erde
ausgelöscht ist meine Qual
mein Hunger ausgetrunken
und mein Herz in Nächten
die zerpflügt sind
mit dem Pflug der Lieder
die Zeit ist ohne End'
doch voll der Träume Not
die mich nicht will
auf meinem Stein des Sterbens.

In Hora Mortis

Time is extinguished
o Lord
my word that came bitter
and dark
Lord
too dark for the earth
my torment is put out
my hunger is drained
and my heart in nights
that are tilled up
with the plow of songs
this time without end
yet filled with the need of dreams
that does not want me
on my headstone.

In Hora Mortis

Morgen Herr bin ich bei Dir
und fern der Welt
die mich nicht braucht
und die mein Korn nicht sät
und nicht mein Leid
das mich betrogen hat
o Herr
mein Gott
ich will jetzt wachsam sein
vor meinem Tod
und vor dem Regen
Herr
der mich jetzt wäscht
aus Furcht
mein Frühling wächst
aus diesem Winter
Herr
mir tropft der Mohn aus Krügen
schwarz
die längst zu Asche sind.

In Hora Mortis

Tomorrow Lord I am by You
and far from the world
that doesn't need me
and that doesn't sow my seed
and my sorrow
that has deceived me
o Lord
my God
I want to be awake now
for my death
and for the rain
Lord
that now washes me
out of fear
that grows my spring
from this winter
Lord
the poppy drips on me from jars
black
that are long since cinders.

In Hora Mortis

IV

Beten will ich auf dem heißen Stein
und die Sterne zählen die im Blut
mir schwimmen
Herr
mein Gott
ich will vergessen sein
nicht mehr fürchte ich den Tag
der morgen kommt
nicht mehr fürchte ich die Nacht
die mich erduldet
Herr
mein Gott
ich fürchte nicht mehr
was noch kommen mag
mein Hunger ist schon ausgelöscht
und die schwarze Qual
ist ausgetrunken.

In Hora Mortis

IV

I want to pray upon the hot stone
and count the stars swimming
in my blood
Lord
my God
I want to be forgotten
I no longer fear the day
that comes tomorrow
I no longer fear the night
that suffers me
Lord
my God
I no longer fear
what may still come
my hunger is already put out
and this black torment
is lapped up.

In Hora Mortis

Preisen will ich Dich mein Gott
in der Verlassenheit
und alle Angst verweht
und jeder Tod schenkt mir der Augen Licht
mein Gott ich preise Dich
wie lang die Zeit auch währt
ich bin nicht mehr allein
bei Dir bin ich
und froh
zerflattert sind die Vögel
schwarz
und wieder
schwarz
die Zahl zerspringt
der Mond schreit auf
ich aber bin
vorbei.

In Hora Mortis

I want to praise You my God
in this solitude
and all fear scatters
and every death gives my eyes light
my God I praise You
for as long as time exists
I am no longer alone
I am by You
and joyful
the birds fly apart
black
and more
black
their number explodes
the moon screams out
but I am
gone.

In Hora Mortis

Herr laß vergessen mich
meine Seele
und der Augen Qual
und müder Lippen Dolch
und grünes Feuer ferner Hütten
jedes Tümpels Maul
vergessen
Herr
mein Gott
den Tag
der mir den Schrei zerspaltet
den ich schrie
und vieler Vögel Zug
zerstückelt ist mein Zorn
und frei mein Blut
in Strömen.

In Hora Mortis

Lord let me forget
my soul
and the agony in my eyes
and the dagger of exhausted lips
and green fires of distant huts
the mouth of each pond
forget
Lord
my God
this day
that splits apart the cry
that I cry
and the passage of countless birds
my anger is dismembered
and my blood flows
in streams.

In Hora Mortis

Die Vögel ach die Vögel
schwarz die Nacht
mein Blut
o Herr
zerschnitten sind mir
alle Vögel
Schrei der gelb
die Zung' verbrennt
zerschnitten
ach im Blut
die Messer Gott
mein Fleisch trink' ich
die Messer
tot ist längst
mein Rot
mein Grün
mein Stachel sticht
zerschnitten
ach
zerschnitten
ach
zerschnitten
ach
ach
ach
mein
Ach.

In Hora Mortis

The birds oh the birds
black the night
my blood
o Lord
are piercing me
all birds
a shriek that yellow
the tongue burning
piercing
oh in the blood
the knives God
I drink my flesh
the knives
long is dead
my red
my green
my thorn sticks
piercing
oh
piercing
oh
piercing
oh
oh
oh
my
Oh.

In Hora Mortis

Unter dem Eisen des Mondes

Under the Iron of the Moon*

*The title is suggested by scene 21 in George Büchner's play *Woyzeck*, in which Marie
observes the redness of the moonrise, and Woyzeck replies, "Wie ein blutig
Eisen" (like a bloody iron or hoop, shackle). This is Bernhard's third book of
verse, which was originally published in 1958 by
Kiepenheuer & Witch,
Cologne.

Das Jahr ist wie das Jahr vor tausend Jahren,
wir tragen den Krug und schlagen den Rücken der Kuh,
wir mähen und wissen nichts vom Winter,
wir trinken Most und wissen nichts,
bald werden wir vergessen sein
und die Verse zerfallen wie Schnee vor dem Haus.

Das Jahr ist wie das Jahr vor tausend Jahren,
wir schauen in den Wald wie in den Stall der Welt,
wir lügen und flechten Körbe für Äpfel und Birnen,
wir schlafen während unsre beschmutzten Schuhe
vor der Haustür verwittern.

Das Jahr ist wie das Jahr vor tausend Jahren,
wir wissen nichts,
wir wissen nichts vom Untergang,
von den versunkenen Städten, vom Strom in dem Pferde
und Menschen ertrunken sind.

Unter dem Eisen des Mondes

The year is like a year a thousand years ago,
we carry the jug and whip behind the cow,
we reap and know nothing of winter,
we drink cider and know nothing,
soon we will be forgotten
and these verses will fall like snow outside the house.

The year is like a year a thousand years ago,
we peer into the woods as if into the cowshed of the world,
we spin lies and weave baskets for apples and pears,
we sleep while our muddy shoes
rot outside the door.

The year is like a year a thousand years ago,
we know nothing,
we know nothing about the end,
about submerged cities, about the stream in which horses
and men are drowning.

Under the Iron of the Moon

Nicht viele sterben
um ein Haus
in der Wüste
oder um einen vertrockneten Baum.

Nicht viele sterben
für Asche
die Feuer war,
für den Wein
eines gestürzten Königs
oder einem Feldherrn
verbrannter Äcker
zur Feier.

Nicht viele sterben
für einen andern,
wenn die Samen wehn
und im Frühling
Tod und Vögel
klare Himmel schwärzen.

Nein,
nicht viele.

Unter dem Eisen des Mondes

Not many die
for a house
in the desert
or a parched tree.

Not many die
for ash
that was fire,
for the wine
of a fallen king
or to toast
some general
of scorched fields.

Not many die
for one another,
when seeds blow in the wind
and in the spring
when death and birds
blacken clear skies.

No,
not many.

Under the Iron of the Moon

Sie werden aufwachen und vergessen sein
im Gelächter das von den Hügeln hereinrollt,
im Gewitter der Wölfe

das ihre Schafsköpfe über den rauchenden Städten zerbläst
zu Staub.
O werde nicht zu Staub

in deinem Hunger unerschöpflich bis zum Rand der Sterne.
Sie werden nachts zu den Sicheln der Verse tanzen
und ihre Augen aufspießen

an der Unsterblichkeit.
O werde nicht zu Staub.
Zieh deine Ruder fest an deine Knochen

und zerschlag den Wind
der weder Ost noch West betrauert,
doch die Qual vernichtet die sie niemals quält.

Unter dem Eisen des Mondes

They will wake up and be forgotten
in the laughter that rolls down from the hills,
in that storm of wolves

that blasts their sheep heads to dust
over the smoking cities.
O don't you become dust

in your hunger extending inexhaustibly to the stars.
They will dance at night to the sickles of verse
and pierce their eyes

on the immortality.
O don't you become dust.
Pull your oars to the bone

and shatter the wind
that mourns neither east nor west,
but the torment never annihilates those it torments.

Under the Iron of the Moon

Der Hahn schreit durch ein Tuch
aus Fleisch und frißt
sich in mein Blut
das mir die Brust
zersägt.

Er trinkt mein Rot
wie einen Mond und lacht,
daß auf den Gipfeln
rot die Sterne
tanzen.

The cock crows through a rag
of skin and gorges
in the blood
that is sawing apart
my chest.

He drinks my color
like a moon and cackles
as the stars
on the mountaintop
dance red.

In den Bergen überfallen die Sterne den stampfenden Regen
wenn du die Lippen meiner Armut anrührst
und unter dem Kirchturm
im winterlichen Brautbett
den Schlag der berstenden Uhr vorausbestimmst.

Die Münder schwelgen im Strom des Weizens,
lautlos schimmern die Bäche
in den Stimmen der Mondnacht
die aus verlassenen Tümpeln steigen
ausgetrunkenen Meeren zu.

Streu den Möwen das Salz deiner Augen,
aber
öffne was du in den niegerochenen Sommern
erstickt hast
und zerfalle im Mund meiner Wunde.

Unter dem Eisen des Mondes

In the mountains stars descend on the driving rain
if you touch my poverty's lips
and underneath the church tower
in a wintry bridal bed
predict the tolling of its bursting clock.

Mouths wallow in the flood of wheat,
soundlessly the brooks shimmer
in the voices of this moonlit night
that rise from deserted ponds
and climb above drained seas.

Scatter the salt of your eyes to the gulls
but
open in summers never scented what you
have smothered
and rot in the mouth of my wound.

Under the Iron of the Moon

Diesen aufgerissenen Himmel im Mund
sterben viele und denken an einen Tag
der auf grünen Tischen
und in kalten Tellern
rosigen Schinkens endete
mit einem Seufzer.

Doch ihre Liebe ist verloren
wie der Wind der die Füße
morscher Bäume
in das Weiß des Nordschnees wickelt.

Ihre Liebe ist verloren
in finsteren Wäldern
die im Schluchzen verirrter Rehe altern
von Wolke zu Wolke.

Unter dem Eisen des Mondes

For this broken sky in their mouth
many die thinking of a day
that ended on green tables
and in cold plates
of pink roast ham
with a sigh.

Yet their love is lost
like the wind winding
around the base of rotted trees
in the white of northern snow.

Their love is lost
in dark forests
grown ancient in the sobs of lost deer
cloud by cloud.

Under the Iron of the Moon

Er allein war am Morgen schon
mit den Vögeln unter dem Himmel
und sagte sich, daß die Hölle grün wird

wenn die Blüten über den Pflöcken treiben.
Er trank aus dem Brunnen der Mutter
und schloß müde Lider auf steinigen Straßen

die unsrer Sprache zeitlebens fremd sind.
Im Sommer wurde er krank
und sah die verrückten Wolken steigen

aus düsteren Träumen,
ein Krieger mit verbrannter Kehle
lag er seine Hand verloren

an die Liebenden zwischen den toten Hügeln,
als der Oktober kam
war er so fremd wie der Schnee

auf den zerschundenen Gipfeln der Berge
und seine Stimme klang hohl
und verdurstet in milchiger Trauer.

Diesen Brief trägt keiner in sein Grab
das winterlich
den steigenden Mond zum Narren hält

auf der Höhe des besungenen Lebens.

Unter dem Eisen des Mondes

In the morning he was already alone
with the birds under the sky
and said to himself that hell is green

when the flowers grow over their stakes.
He drank from the well of his mother
and shut his tired eyes on stone streets

somewhere else in our language all our lives.
In the summer he was sick
and saw the moving clouds rise

out of his dismal dreams,
a soldier with a burning throat,
he laid his hand in vain

on the lovers between the dead hills,
when October came
he was as strange as the snow

on the broken peaks of the mountains,
and his voice sounded hollow
and parched in his milk-white grief.

No one carries this letter to his grave
that in winter
makes a fool of the moon rising

to the height of this life praised to the skies.

Under the Iron of the Moon

Die weißen Blüten meines Frühlings
blühn im Blut,
nur Trauer weht mein Sterben durch die Wüsten,
nur singend schreibt das Gras im Himmel Lieder
wo schwere Wolken weinen düsterer Tage März,
nicht mehr wird uns ein Ohr im Fluß und kein Gebet
im Stein,
der Ruderer der Sterne stirbt,
die blauen Esel gehen mit leeren Krügen heiter
durch das braune Laub.
Wann wird mein Gott mir sagen wo und wann
die Zeit den Stachel treibt ins Fleisch?
Mir brennt die Nacht die Stunden aus,
Gemäuer plündert mir das Herz,
ich will verwehn,
mein Frost hängt mit den Blättern, Schlaf in fremden
Häusern,
irr im Tal bohrt sich das Licht in mein Gebet
aus Müdigkeit,
und Geist erhebt den Sommer,
auf dem Grab den Tod
wo meiner wunden Lippen kranke Sonnen ziehn
über die grüne Welt mit Schläfern roter Asche
ein Tuch aus Mond und Milch und Wind und Tränen.

Unter dem Eisen des Mondes

The white flowers of my spring
blossom in blood,
only grief blows my dying through the wastes,
only the grass singing into the sky writes songs
where heavy clouds weep somber March days,
we no longer are an ear in the river and a prayer
in the stone,
the rower of the stars dies,
and through the brown leaves
blue donkeys walk serenely with their empty jugs.
When will my God tell me where and when
time gets to drive its thorn into my flesh?
My hours are burnt out by the night,
crumbling walls plunder my heart,
I want to blow away,
my frost clings to the leaves, my sleep in strange houses,
the light in my prayer bores itself insanely into the valley
from exhaustion,
and a ghost is raised in the summer,
the dead upon their grave
where the diseased suns of my bleeding lips pull
across the green world with its sleepers of red ash
a sheet of moon and milk and wind and tears.

Under the Iron of the Moon

Meine Verzweiflung kommt um Mitternacht
und schaut mich an als wär ich lange tot
die Augen schwarz und müd die Stirn vor Blüten,
der bittere Honig meiner Traurigkeit
tropft auf die kranke Erde nieder
die mich in roten Nächten wachhält oft
zu sehn des Herbstes unruhvolles Sterben.

Meine Verzweiflung kommt um Mitternacht
aus den verworrenen Träumen der Sonne und des Regens,
früh sag ich, daß ich alles lobte
und fremd bin meiner Tür und meiner Angst,
vieltausend Jahre stürzen aus den kalten Wänden
und tragen mich ein Stück dem Winter zu.

Meine Verzweiflung kommt um Mitternacht
verändert ist das Tal, der Mond schwimmt auf den Wiesen,
des zornigen Abends zerbrochene Sichel lehnt
am Fensterbrett und schaut mich an.
Ich weiß genau, daß ich zerschlagen bin
wie diese Sichel, keiner täuscht mich jetzt,
auch nicht der Fluß der seinen Spruch
noch vor dem Morgen fällt.

Unter dem Eisen des Mondes

My despair comes at midnight
and I look on as though I were long dead
the black eyes and the brow tired of flowers,
the bitter honey of my grief
drips on this sick earth
that so often keeps me awake on red nights
to see autumn's restless dying.

My despair comes at midnight
out of confused dreams of sun and rain,
in the morning I admit that I praise everything,
that I am a stranger to my own door and fear,
many thousands of years slide down the cold walls
and carry me a bit more toward winter.

My despair comes at midnight,
the valley has changed, the moon floats on the meadow,
the angry evening rests its broken sickle
against the windowsill and regards me.
I am quite sure that I am as broken
as this sickle, no one is going to deceive me now,
not even the river still uttering its sentence
before morning comes.

Under the Iron of the Moon

Unter dem Baum und unter dem Fluß bist du mir fremd.
Du, auf der Seite der unerträglichen Sonne,
schwarze Nacht, vertraut dem Tier
in aufgerissenen Wäldern,
ratlos meiner Liebe
die dem schwimmenden Mond entgegen taumelt,
gekränkt unter Brombeersträuchern,
über den Wurzeln lachend, wie
eine Schlange zischend
unter dem Schlag meines Stockes,
durstig an den Hängen,

o meiner Mutter Traum bis ins Mark der Erde,
diese Verlassenheit in des Sommers singenden Ketten,
Haar aus Asche, verdorrt
sind deine Glieder und in den Mörtel
meiner Trauer gebrannt für immer,
bis die Erinnerung ihren heiligen Schnee
in die knirschenden Täler schickt
und der Frost Lieder und Wünsche
erstarren läßt in der zitternden Luft.

Du, der ich treu war über einen Winter,
durch das Feuer des Sommers hörte ich
dich rufen—falscher Augen Blitz,
zerstöre mich im Winkel deines Herzens.

Unter dem Eisen des Mondes

Under the tree and in the river you are strange to me.
You, at the side of the unbearable sun,
black night, trusting the beast
in gashed forests,
my helpless love
that reels toward the floating moon,
sickened under the blackberry bushes,
over the roots laughing like
a snake hissing
under the blow of my stick,
thirsty on the hillsides,

o my mother's dream in the marrow of the earth,
this loneliness in summer's singing chains,
hair of ash, your limbs
are withered and burned into the mortar
of my grief forever,
until memory sends its sacred snow
into those valleys gnashing together
and the frost freezes songs and desires
stiff in the cold air.

You, to whom I was faithful over a winter,
I heard you calling
through the fire of the summer
—lightning of lying eyes,
destroy me in the corner of your heart.

Under the Iron of the Moon

Der Schläfer ist im Himmel und in der Hölle
zu Hause und hört Orgeln
aus Blüten und trinkt Staub
von winterlichen Gliedern.

Seine Gelübde sterben in Wäldern,
auf trockenen Stämmen
schließt er auf was war und geht
hinunter frierend in die versoffenen Täler.

In hohlen Häusern treibt sein Hirn den Stachel
in fließendes Fleisch verbotener Liebe.
Unheimlich kehrt er in den Morgen
zurück und hält noch vieler Toter Traum in seinen Händen.

Unter dem Eisen des Mondes

The sleeper is at home in heaven and hell
and hears the organs
in flowers and drinks dust
from wintry limbs.

His vows perish in the forests,
to barren trees
he discloses what was and walks
down freezing into the drunken valleys.

In empty houses his brain drives the thorn
into the smooth flesh of forbidden love.
Unearthly he returns in the morning
and still keeps that dream of so many dead in his hands.

Under the Iron of the Moon

Unter des Feuers Atem sträubt
sich dein Arm
in den versunkenen Tälern,
mit frühen Morgen schmückt
sich die steigende Sonne deiner Glieder
und gräbt sich in die Lippen tiefer als die Nacht.

Nicht länger ist zwischen uns die Erde
trauriger Stunden Asche
vor verrosteten Türen,
als ein verwilderter Wind in Träumen
deiner wunden Lider Schweigen öffnet
und dieses Herz Baum wird und Qual
und Honig tropft von winterlichen Dächern,
süßer Schnee von den Stirnen der Welt
für einen Augenblick stürzender Liebe
von Blut zu Blut
an den Ufern überschäumender Apfelbäume
in den Ketten des Frühlings
der mich allein lassen wird
mit einer berstenden Brust voll Qual.

Unter dem Eisen des Mondes

Amid the fire's breath
you raise your arm
in these sunken valleys,
with early morning
the rising sun of your limbs adorns itself
and buries itself inside these lips deeper than night.

That earth of miserable hours
is no longer cinders between us
from rusted doors
as a wind running wild in dreams
opens the silence of your wounded lids
and this heart becomes a tree and pain
and honey drips from wintry roofs,
sweet snow from the world's brow
for one moment of love streaming
blood to blood
on these shores white-capped with apple blossoms
inside these chains of spring
that will leave me alone
with a breast bursting with agony.

Under the Iron of the Moon

Der Regen dieser Tage
geht nur bis zum verrosteten Herzen der Nacht
in die finsteren Gänge der Toten

die mit Fledermäusen unter den Balken hängen
und mit knarrenden Fingern
Engel in die Finsternis zeichnen zwischen den Sternen

die über den Schweinen tanzen und Kühe verfolgen
in ihren unruhigen Schlaf
mit Stöhnen und Raunen der Milch zwischen weißen
                                        Gliedern.

Oft einer streckt sein verlassenes Bein aus dem Bett
und läßt Kinn und Welt träumen
auf den staubigen Bohlen des Lasters

wo der Mond vor der Leinwand erzittert
in mühsamen Sprüchen unbeschützter Schwestern
die Gott loben im süßen Brot und in langen Speckseiten

bis der Wein ihre Hirne anfüllt mit Himmeln
die aus Asche sind und das Gras
ihre verkommenen Füße einrollt

sie schwimmen auf gelben Brüsten
durch die Vergänglichkeit trauriger Frühlinge
Mädchen in schwarzen Mänteln voll Apfelduft

von ihren staunenden Mündern aus Armut
fließen die verrückten Klagen
über mein Gesicht aus Stein und Tränen.

Unter dem Eisen des Mondes

70

The rain of these days
reaches only to the night's rusted heart
in the black passages of the dead

who hang with bats under the beams
and with scraping fingers
make angels in the darkness between the stars

dancing over pigs, dogging the cows
in their restless sleep
with their lowing and the sigh of milk between
                                        white legs.

Often one stretches his one lone limb out in bed
and lets chin and world dream
on the dusty planks of vice

where the moon shudders before the linen screen
in the tiring patter of unguarded sisters
who praise God in sugar bread and in long slivers of bacon

until wine fills their brains with skies
made of ash and the grass
curls in their depraved feet

floundering on sallow breasts
through the passing of doleful springs
of girls in black coats and apples smelling

from their astonished mouths of poverty
that pour these demented moans
over my face of stone and tears.

Under the Iron of the Moon

Horch, im Wind wehn
Ängste,
vieler Kinder Augen
schließen sich
in unruhvollen Bächen.
Wilder klagt
der Vogel
meines Sterbens,
horch,
im Wind wehn
Ängste,
fröstelnd kehrt
was mir verloren war
zurück,
im Tod stehn viele auf
mit wunden Händen
weiße Segel
haltend
müder Sterne
und beweinter Sommer,
horch, mein Bruder
Schwester,
horch,
im Wind wehn
Ängste.

Unter dem Eisen des Mondes

Listen, fears blow
in the wind,
the eyes of many children
close in streams full
of restlessness.
The bird of
my death
cries wilder,
listen,
fears blow
in the wind,
what I lost
comes shivering
back,
in death, many raise
white sails
with wounded hands
holding
tired stars
and mourned summers,
listen, my brother
sister,
listen,
fears blow
in the wind.

Under the Iron of the Moon

Schlaf neben mir, sei ruhig ich muß trauern,
beginn ich wieder meine Reise, zähl ich Stern
und Kraut im Moor und suchend deine Lieder
erwecke ich die Furcht in meiner Qual
die meiner Stimme keine Ufer gibt
    und meinem Mund kein Wort.

Bleib bei den Ängsten und zerfall zu Staub,
auf finstern Treppen schlag dich offenen Augs,
in mein Gebet schließ ich dich ein wie nur die Mutter,
liebend weißen Mond und nackte Rippen kalter Wälder.

O komm nicht in mein Gehen nach düsteren Träumen.
Sag, wo war ich gestern? War ich dir nicht nah
als ich zufrieden lag am Brunnenrand
aufschüttend fremder Gräber trockene Erde
und kaltem Wind nachgebend
längst verwehter Spuren Sand auf meinen Schuhn?
Sag?
    Du verstehst mich nicht.
Schlaf neben mir, sei ruhig ich muß trauern.

Unter dem Eisen des Mondes

Sleep beside me, be quiet I must grieve,
I begin my journey all over, I count star
and plant in the moor and seeking your songs
in my agony I wake the fear
that gives my voice no limit,
    my mouth no word.

Keep to your fears and crumble into dust,
cover your open eyes on dark stairs,
I include you in my prayers just like my mother,
loving the white moon and the naked ribs of cold forests.

In my going after black dreams, O don't come.
Tell me, where was I yesterday? Was I not with you
as I lay happy by the edge of the fountain
spewing the dry soil of foreign graves
and cold wind giving way
to sand of long-obliterated tracks on my shoes?
Well?
    You don't understand me.
Sleep beside me, be quiet I must grieve.

Under the Iron of the Moon

Die Toten haben das Land gerichtet
und den Äckern Frieden und Unrast gegeben
und der Sonne den Hügel und den Wäldern die Finsternis
die uns morgen heimsuchen wird.
Verlassen sind unsere Unterstände. Tausend Frühlinge ziehn
von den Meeren herein in die Mutter.

Unter dem Eisen des Mondes

The dead have turned the soil
and given peace and unrest to the fields
and the sun to the hill and the darkness to the woods
that will haunt us tomorrow.
The holes we dug are deserted. A thousand springs drawn
by the seas are here in your mother.

Under the Iron of the Moon

Von Morgen zu Morgen
sprich mit Gott
über die Freuden
und deiner Kinder Ängste
im Rad der Vergänglichkeit.

Dort auch ergrauen
im Krater
die Sünden,
was war,
Tod und Feuer
unter dem Staub
der verschlossenen Tür.
In längst vergessenen Meeren
schwimmen die Sterne
deiner Verzweiflung.
Lautlos schaut
aus den Gräsern
der zerbrochene Frühling
der Toten.

Über dem Feuer
züngelt ein Feuer
des Jubels,
unter den Dächern
staubiger Höfe
und sanfter Kapellen.
Aus den Särgen der Nacht
steigt der wütende Mond,
trauriger Wiesen und kranke
das Leichentuch des Winters ziehend
über bleiche Schultern
trauriger Wiesen und kranker Bäche.

Unter dem Eisen des Mondes

Morning by morning
talk to God
about the joys
and the fears of your children.
in that wheel of mortality.

In the crater
the sins there
turn gray too,
what was,
death and fire
under the dust
of the locked door.
In long-forgotten seas
swim the stars
of your despair.
The broken spring
of the dead
watches silently
from the grass.

Above the fire
lick the flames
of jubilation,
under the roofs
of dusty inns
and quiet chapels.
From the coffins of the night
the angry moon climbs,
pulling the winding sheet of winter
over the pale shoulders
of grieving meadows and ailing streams.

Under the Iron of the Moon

Die Nacht zerfällt an Toren alter Mauern,
unruhig hängt der Mond, die Erde sucht
des letzten Sommers Frost sich zu erhalten
und auf den Bergen stehn die Sterne weiß,
mit grünen Augen blicken stumm
herab der Bäume müd gewordene Lider.

Ich bring Verachtung in das Tal und viele sagen,
daß ich nur Tod und Traum und Eifersucht
in großen Körben trage für den Untergang.
Die Sterne fluchen! Seltsam fällt der Tag
in seine Furchen nah dem Fluß der weit
hinunter in die Phantasien fließt
mit strengen Sprüchen meines Wintertages.

Unter dem Eisen des Mondes

The night falls against the gates of old walls,
the moon floats restlessly, the earth seeks
to hold on to last summer's frost
and stars are white on the mountains,
with green eyes, with weary lids
the trees stare silently downward.

I bring contempt into the valley and many say
that I bear only death and dreams and jealousy
in great baskets for the end of the world.
The stars curse! The day falls strangely
into its furrows by the river flowing
away in these fantasies
with my winter's harsh verdicts.

Under the Iron of the Moon

Das blanke Eisen des Mondes
wird dich töten und der starre
Fuß eines Riesenvogels
dem du
deine Trauer anvertraut hast
im Winter.

Der Wald wird seine Knochen
in Unruhe wickeln,
und dich niederwerfen
der Wind
der aus dem weißen Versteck
zerfallener Rehe
zustößt.

Die Sonne wird ihr Wundenmal
vergraben
hinter den sterbenden Stämmen
und deiner Lippen Feuer
flammen
zu lachenden Blüten
des Todes.

The bright iron of the moon
will kill you and the numb
talons of a giant bird
in whom
you confided your grief
during the winter.

The forest will wind its bones
in restlessness
and the wind
will beat you to the ground,
striking
from the white hiding-place
of rotting deer.

The sun will bury the mark
of its wounds
beyond the dying trees
and your lips of fire
will flame
into laughing flowers
of death.

Under the Iron of the Moon

Dein Grab
wird im Süden
gegraben,
dein Tod
wird im Süden
wehn,
dein Gesicht
ist von Disteln zerrissen,
dein Krug
ist von Vögeln zerstört.

Dein Grab
wird im Süden
gegraben,
dein Tod
wird im Süden
wehen.
Dein Tal
wird dich vergessen.
Du kommst
nicht mehr.

Unter dem Eisen des Mondes

Your grave
will be dug
in the south,
your death
will blow
in the south,
your face
is scratched open by thistles,
your wine cup
is broken by birds.

Your grave
will be dug
in the south,
your death
will blow
in the south.
Your valley
will forget you.
You come
no more.

Under the Iron of the Moon

Versuche nicht, mein Lob zu singen
und meine Armut
hinter den Flügelschlägen des Herbstes zu preisen.
Versuche nicht, meinem verworfenen Glück
und meiner geräderten Stimme
die Angst aus den Fingern zu stoßen.
Versuche nicht, mich zu trösten,
denn der Winter gehört mir allein
mit den Schritten des Schnees
und dem Klirren verstreuter Hufe
und dem Uhrwerk in meiner Brust
das nichts von sterbenden Städten weiß.

Versuche nicht, meiner Zahl Hügel und Flüsse
zu rauben die des Sommers Gefährten sind.
Versuche nicht, das Gras, das mein Gebrechen singt
unter dem Messer meiner Pflugschar,
aufzuspalten für eine Verzweiflung aus Asche
und einen verkommenen Schluck
aus dem Tal dieses unbegreiflichen Volkes
das ohne Meer und ohne Gewissen ist.

Unter dem Eisen des Mondes

Don't try to sing my praise
and praise my destitution
after the wingbeats of autumn.
Don't try to poke out my sick pleasure
and the drained voice
of my fear with your finger.
Don't try to console me,
for the winter belongs to me alone,
with footprints in the snow,
with the crunching of scattering hooves,
with the clockwork in my chest
that knows nothing about dying cities.

Don't try to steal from my count of hills and rivers
that are the summer's companions.
Don't try to split the grass singing of my affliction
under the blade of my plow
for some despair made of ashes
and a decaying mouthful
from the valley of these incomprehensible people
who are without a sea and without a conscience.

Under the Iron of the Moon

Mir scheint, daß ich viel jünger war
jünger noch als die schon starben,
Städte sah ich und der Augen Müdigkeit
war des Sommers Klagen in den Bächen.

Jünger war ich als die mich oft kränkten
und die meinen Namen längst vergessen haben
hinterm Webstuhl, unterm Hammer,
oder in dem schroffen Zug der Egge.

Mir scheint, daß ich viel jünger war
und im März mit Wolken hing am Himmel,
Märkte bauend ohne Totenmähler

und verkohlte Herzen,
auch mit dem April war ich auf Reisen
zog mit Vögeln Flüsse abwärts,

lachte unter Büschen
und war mit den Gräsern traurig.
In den Zimmern sah ich

viele sterben die mich liebten.
Mit dem Wind zu sprechen aber
war ich auserwählt.

Mir scheint, daß ich viel jünger war,
wilde Totenmessen roch ich,
wilde Sterne,

Kirchen standen auf im Meer des Weizens,
immer war
die Wange meines Hügels

Unter dem Eisen des Mondes

To me I was much younger,
younger than those who had already died,
I saw cities and the strain in my eyes
was summer's crying in the streams.

I was younger than the ones who so often hurt me
and who have long forgotten my name
behind the loom, under the hammer,
or in the sharp pull of the harrow.

To me I was much younger,
and caught up with the clouds in the March sky,
fairs setting up without wakes for the dead

and hearts burned black,
and with April I journeyed out,
drifting down rivers with the birds,

laughing amid bunches of flowers
and grieving with the grass.
In the rooms I saw

many perishing away who cherished me.
But I chose to speak
to the wind.

To me I was much younger,
I could smell the savage requiem masses,
the savage stars,

the churches standing in a sea of wheat,
the cheek of my hill
always knew

Under the Iron of the Moon

meinem Zorn vertraut.
So müde war ich nur
wo Äpfel klangen und der Winter sang

aus tausend Muscheln.
Seufzend ging der Tag,
das Jahr stand an der Mauer
schwärzlich, von den Ängsten meiner Zeit verstört.

Mir scheint, daß ich viel jünger war.

Unter dem Eisen des Mondes

my anger firsthand.
I was just so tired
where apples tolled and winter sang

from a thousand mussel shells.
The day passed sighing,
the year stood on the wall
all black, disturbed by the fears of my time.

To me I was much younger.

Under the Iron of the Moon

Hinter dem schwärzlichen Wald
brechen meine Gedanken die Zelte ab.
Das zerborstene Schaukelpferd
des Sommers hat der Mond
in den Schnee gestellt.
Auf einem silbernen Schweif sitzt
die verlorene Sonne
und späht herab auf die hilflosen Dörfer
die allein geblieben sind
mit dem Most der Krieger
und mit der Erde der Angst.

Dich schützt nur die Schlange des Ruhms
die ihr Grün unter faulen Blättern verspritzt
und sich zurückzieht
unter der kalten Fackel der Nacht.

Unter dem Eisen des Mondes

From behind the black woods
my thoughts strike their tents.
The moon has chased down
the smashed rocking horse of summer
into the snow.
The lost sun
perches on a silver tail
and peers down on the helpless villages
that have persisted all alone
on the cider of the brave
and the soil of fear.

Only the serpent of fame protects you,
spitting its green among the rotting leaves
and retreating
under the cold torch of the night.

Under the Iron of the Moon

Der Stein spricht von den Sünden
zwischen dem Feuer der Insel
und dem Scheitern der Nacht.

Die Geborgenen haben ein Kleid
aus Ruhm um ihr Fleisch gewickelt
und den Honig der Toten
in ihrer zweifachen Brust verwahrt.

Hinter dem Gras und hinter der Stadt
die von den Gedanken erzittert
schlafen die scheuen Kinder,
träumen die schwarzen Hunde
die mich heimsuchen früh im April.

Der Stein spricht von den Sünden
zwischen dem Feuer der Insel
und dem Scheitern der Nacht.

Unter dem Eisen des Mondes

The stone speaks of sins
between the fire of the island
and the shipwreck of the night.

The charmed lives have a suit
of success to cover their bodies
and the honey of the dead
hoarded in their double breast.

Beyond the grass and the city
trembling about these thoughts,
shy children sleep,
the black dogs dream,
the ones that attack me early in April.

The stone speaks of sins
between the fire of the island
and the shipwreck of the night.

Under the Iron of the Moon

Mein Gebet hört Gott auch
am Morgen im Kornfeld
wo der Wind
die Kinder des Mittags sammelt
und die Entschlafenen
von ihren Gehirnen ausruhen
an der Mauer.
Gott hört mich
in der Finsternis des Regens
und auf den Wegen
bittrer Gräser und blanker Steine
über den Totenschädeln der Nacht
die in meinen Träumen zerschellen
aus Furcht.
Gott hört mich
in jedem Winkel der Welt.

Unter dem Eisen des Mondes

God hears my prayer too
in the morning, in the cornfield
where the wind
gathers the children of the afternoon
and the departed
rest their tired minds
on the wall.
God hears me
in the darkness of the rain
and on that path
of bitter grass and shining stones
across the skulls of night
that are smashed apart in my dreams
out of fear.
God hears me
in every corner of the world.

Under the Iron of the Moon

Der Frühling ist dein Totenbett.
In die Münder schäumender Büsche
kehrst du zurück.
Von deinen Kindern bleibt dir kein Weinen
und von den Männern kein Schatten
im widerspenstigen Haar.
Das Licht zieht deine Lüge durch die Felder,
die Spuren wilder Verzweiflung
schwärzen dein Gesicht
das auf einer häßlichen Wolke
aus Leinwand liegt.
Viele Wälder zerfielen zu Asche
unter dem Feuer deiner zornigen Seele.

Unter dem Eisen des Mondes

The spring is your deathbed.
In the foaming mouths of the bushes
you come back.
From your children no tears are left for you
and from the men no shadows
          in your unkempt hair.
The light drags your lies through the fields,
the tracks of wild despair
blacken your face
that lies on the hideous cloud
of a sheet.
Many forests turn to ash
amid the fire of your angry soul.

Under the Iron of the Moon

Kein Baum und kein Himmel
wird dich trösten,
auch nicht das Mühlrad
hinter dem Krachen des Tannenholzes,
kein sterbender Vogel,
nicht die Eule und nicht das rasende Rebhuhn,

zurück ist es weit,

dich wird kein Strauch mehr schützen
vor kalten Sternen
und blutigen Zweigen,
kein Baum und kein Himmel
wird dich trösten,
in den Kronen zerborstener Winter
wächst dein Tod
mit steifen Fingern
fern von Gras und Wildnis
in die Sprüche des frisch gefallenen Schnees.

Unter dem Eisen des Mondes

No tree and no sky
will console you,
not the millwheel
after pine logs are split,
no dying bird,
not the owl, not the scurrying partridge,

it's a long way back,

the thicket will no longer protect you
from the cold stars
and bloody branches,
no tree and no sky
will console you,
in the crown of the shattered winter
your death grows
with frozen fingers
far from the grass and wilderness
in the verses of freshly fallen snow.

Under the Iron of the Moon

Hinter dem schwarzen Wald
verbrenne ich dieses Feuer meiner Seele
in dem der Atem der Städte flackert
und die Amsel der Angst.
Mit bloßen Händen erschlage ich diese Flammen
die der Luft ins Gehirn steigen
und in meinem Namen zittern.
Als Wolke zieht mein Herz
über die Dächer
nah den Flüssen
bis ich, ein später Regen, wiederkehre
tief im Herbst.

Unter dem Eisen des Mondes

Beyond this black forest
I stoke this fire of my soul
flickering with the breathing of the cities
and the blackbirds of fear.
With bare hands I kill these flames
that climb the air into my brain
and shiver in my name.
My heart drifts as a cloud
over the rooftops
along the rivers,
until I return, a later rain
deep in the fall.

Under the Iron of the Moon

Der letzte Tag ist im Bierkrug
und in Verzweiflung gefangen,
er wächst mit den Vögeln hinter dem Haus
und stürzt in den schwarzen Tümpel.
Kein Schrei hält diese Hände,
diese zerschundenen Hände
und dieses aufbegehrende Herz.

Die Schatten schreiben April und Dezember
über dem Türbalken auf
und reden von Bäumen und kranken Mädchen
und zerstören den Spruch
im rosigen Schinkenblatt.

Der letzte Tag ist im Bierkrug
und in Verzweiflung gefangen.

Unter dem Eisen des Mondes

The last day is trapped
in this beer glass and despair,
it mounts with the birds behind the house
and plunges into the black pond.
No scream stops these hands,
these raw hands
and this angry heart.

The shadows write up April and December
over the door
and discuss trees and diseased girls
and ruin their inscription
in a pink slice of ham.

The last day is trapped
in this beer glass and despair.

Under the Iron of the Moon

Unmerklich weht der Wind
über das Land.
Schon stellt der Winter mich
im hohen Norden
und wirft mich in
sein schweigendes Gewand.

Von späten Ernten trifft
der Frost mich wieder.
Du stehst nicht auf.
Du redest nur im Zorn.
Mich stürzt im Herbst
der Hunger deiner Glieder.

Im Schlaf verteilt die Nacht
die großen Orden
der Vergänglichkeit.
Mich rührt kein Traum.
Vorm Fenster hör ich nachts
den Tod im Baum.

O dieser Frühling
der zerschlagen liegt.
O dieser Sommer, tot,
auf weißen Kissen.
Den düstern Herbst hab ich
in dir besiegt
und eine Tür zum Winter
aufgerissen.
Die späten Nächte fürcht ich
lang und klar.
Verbittert such ich jetzt
im Park, was war.

Unter dem Eisen des Mondes

The wind blows imperceptibly
across the land.
and already the winter corners me
in the high north
and hurls me into
its silent robe.

Once more I feel the frost
of late harvests.
You don't get up.
You speak only in anger.
The hunger of your limbs
plunges me into autumn.

During sleep the night
hands out the great medals
of ephemeralness.
No dream moves me.
Outside the window each night
I hear death in the trees.

O this spring
that lies broken.
O this summer, dead,
on white pillows.
I have overcome
the somber autumn in you
and flung open
the door to winter.
I fear the late nights,
long and clear.
I search bitterly now
in the park for what was.

Under the Iron of the Moon

Komm unter den Baum, dort richten
die Toten sich auf, die stolzen Münder der Nacht,
und das weiße Gebein stellt in Träumen
den verschlafenen Mond an der Mauer.

Der Frühling fließt mit dem Strom der Glieder
hinunter in die Zerbrechlichkeit wilder Vögel
die an den Ufern warten auf ihre verzweifelten Flüge
wo die Stimmen der Wolken sich ballen
und in den Zweigen ertrunkene Kinder
        in grünen Kränzen schlafen.

Die Winde sind alt geworden und die Lippen,
bevor aus dem Tal die Botschaft zu sterben kommt
trennen sich Sonne und Mund für immer
und still geht auf singenden Stöcken die Zeit des Sommers

zurück in das Totenhaus
aus dem der Mond aufgestiegen ist mit müden Augen
hinter den schwarzen Fingern des Waldes.

Unter dem Eisen des Mondes

Come under the tree, there the dead
sit up, the proud mouths of night,
and in dreams the white skeleton
places the still-sleeping moon on the wall.

Spring flows down with that stream of limbs
into the fragility of wild birds
waiting on the banks for their desperate soaring,
where the voices of the clouds gather
and the drowned children in the branches sleep
      in green rosaries.

The winds are getting old and so are the lips,
before the message from the valley comes to die
the sun and mouth split forever
and the time of summer creeps up singing vines

back into the house of the dead
from which the moon has risen with its tired eyes
behind the black fingers of the forest.

Under the Iron of the Moon

Bevor der Winter mich überfällt
hinter den feindlichen Höfen
die ihre Musik mit Schnee zudecken und süßem Rauch

—eingeschlafen sind die Kinder und Hunde
unter des Baches Müdigkeit,
auch die Amsel vergißt dich und der Krug,
düsterer Jahre Geruch in stummen Gärten
führt Gespräche mit Baum und Schatten—,

will ich dem Schlaf die Schuhe hinstellen
und die Mühsal des langen Krieges vergessen
und meinem Bruder begegnen auf dem Friedhof
zur abendlichen Trauer zwischen zwei Grabsteinen,
dem des Vaters und dem der Mutter,
und das Wehn des Weizens über dem Totenhügel
herein lassen in meinen Psalm von der Erde
die uns begraben wird mit Furcht und Hohn
unter den träumenden Gliedern der Sonne.

Unter dem Eisen des Mondes

Before winter attacks me
behind those farmhouses of my enemies
that conceal their music with snow and sweet smoke

—the dogs and children sleep
under rivers of weariness,
the blackbird forgets you and the wine cup,
in silent gardens the smell of somber years
holds conversations with tree and shade—

I want to put my shoes to sleep
and forget the troubles of the long war
and meet my brother at the cemetery
for the evening's grieving between two gravestones,
one our father's and one our mother's,
and let the wind in the wheat over the mounds
enter my psalm of the earth
that will bury us with fear and scorn
beneath the dreaming limbs of the sun.

Under the Iron of the Moon

Die Krähenfüße des Winters laß mich sehen
und deine Augen die zu erdrosselten Amseln
geworden sind
und das Herz das du auf dem Acker ausgesetzt hast,
damit es die Messer der Flügel singen hört.

Den Abend laß mich zerfallen sehen vor deinem Gesicht
das nie mehr zurückkehren kann in das Haus
in dem die Böcke der Weihnacht lachen
unter den Spritzern deines verbitterten Blutes.

Die Stimme laß mich hören die in den Bäumen kein Echo
                                        findet
und im Tal um die Höfe hallt
ohne den vergeßnen Hahn zu trösten oder die zerstörte
                                        Mutter.

Den Tümpel zeig mir aus dem dein Zorn steigt
mit roten Augen und einem Käfig für deine Lieder
in der zerschlagenen Hand.

Unter dem Eisen des Mondes

Let me see the crow's feet of winter
and your eyes that changed into strangled blackbirds
and that heart that you have exposed in the field
so that it hears those knives of wings sing.

Let me see the evening decay before your face
that can never go back inside the house
in which the buck goats of Christmas Eve laugh
amid the spurting of your embittered blood.

Let me hear the voice that finds no echo in the trees
and resounds around the farms in the valley
without the consolation of the forgotten rooster or the
                                              destroyed mother.

The pond shows me where your anger rises
with red eyes and a birdcage for your songs
in this worn-out hand.

Under the Iron of the Moon

Nah ist der Tod mir jetzt und nah der Winter,
Unruhe träumt das Tal und hält mich wach
und mancher Wind der auf erfrorene Dächer
der Tage und der Nächte Namen schreibt.

Wieder im Meer des wunderbaren Weizens
bin ich von strengen Flügen müd zurück
zuhörend noch den Reden alter Mauern,
doch fern dem Zorn der nie geliebten Städte.

In alten Liedern und zerbrochenen Augen
wo scheu der Mond die dunklen Ernten treibt
will ich der Toten tief vergrabene Sonne
auf grünen Hügeln sehn in fremden Himmeln

und früher Sommer Staub im Abendwind.

Unter dem Eisen des Mondes

Death and winter are near me now,
the valley dreams restlessly and keeps me up
as does a wind writing the names of these days
and nights on the frozen roofs.

I am back in that sea of wonderful wheat
once again, tired from my strenuous flying,
still listening to the talk of old walls,
yet far from the fury of those cities never loved.

In old songs and ruined eyes,
where the moon timidly drives the dark harvests,
I want to see the buried deep sun of the dead
on green hills, in strange skies

and the early summer's dust in the evening wind.

Under the Iron of the Moon

Vergiß mich in den Zimmern,
lösch mich aus vorm Tor,
laß Schnee von weißen Gipfeln treiben
in mein Altern,
o vergiß mich,

langsam wird mein Tod
im Süden Städte streifen
mit dem Wind die Türme froher Tage,
o vergiß mich,

ich bin längst vorbei im März
und mit dem Spruch des Baums
der täglich stirbt
hinter den Bergen
schneebedeckt,
vergiß mich,

morgen ist von gestern
nur der Rauch
von tausend Mündern
schwarzer Dächer,
Tod,
vergiß mich.

O vergiß mich
winterlich in Tälern,
trüben Herzen zugewandt
und Träumen
wie der Möwe Flügelschlag
der Nacht.

Unter dem Eisen des Mondes

Forget me in these rooms,
extinguish me before the gate,
let snow from white mountain peaks
drift in my old age,
o forget me,

my death will slowly
wander with the wind
in the south cities, towers of happier days,
o forget me,

in March I am long gone,
up in the mountains,
and covered with snow
with the verdict of the trees
dying each day,
forget me,

tomorrow is only smoke
from yesterday
from a thousand mouths
of black rooftops,
death,
forget me.

O forget me
each winter in the valleys,
loyal to my grim heart
and dreams
like seagulls' wingbeats
at night.

Under the Iron of the Moon

Der November kam überall
   überall
aus frierenden Wäldern

traurige Musik vor ausgehöhlten
   Gräbern
zueinander redend

bis der Mond spät sinkend
   überm Kirchturm
seinen Schleier zuzog.

Der November kam überall
   überall
vielleicht daß auf der Wange

der Schnee schmilzt wenn die
   Glocken
den Frost durcheinander schütteln

und durch das schimpfende Meer unsere
   Morgen
blicken in die unbewegliche Muschel des Frühlings.

Unter dem Eisen des Mondes

November came everywhere
    everywhere
from freezing forests

a sad music before hollowed-out
    graves
conversing with each other

until the moon, sinking late
    over the church tower,
drew its veil.

November came everywhere
    everywhere
so that the snow melts by some chance

on our cheek when the
    bells
rattle through the frost

and our mornings peer through the swearing
    sea
into the motionless seashell of spring.

Under the Iron of the Moon

Eine Blume,
eine weiße Blume
hat meinen Zorn getrunken
in der verlorenen Stadt
und will von Wolken und Bäumen
nichts mehr wissen.

In ihren Augen verwelken die Kinder
unruhigen Fleisches
und trauriger Lieder
die nicht mehr zu singen sind.

Wo soll ich diese verzweifelte Stunde aufhängen,
diese Stunde die mich auslöscht
bevor der Schnee die Zungen
und die Rosen der Einöde
unter dem zerrissenen Weiß erstickt?

Eine Blume,
eine weiße Blume
hat meinen Zorn getrunken
in der verlorenen Stadt
und will von Wolken und Bäumen
nichts mehr wissen.

Unter dem Eisen des Mondes

A flower,
a white flower
has sipped my anger
in this forsaken city
and wants to know nothing more
about clouds and trees.

In its eyes wilt the children
of restless flesh
and sad songs
that are not sung anymore.

Where shall I hang this desperate hour,
this hour that crushes me out
before the snow sticks to tongues
and to the roses of the barrens
torn through the white?

A flower,
a white flower
has sipped my anger
in this forsaken city
and wants to know nothing more
about clouds and trees.

Under the Iron of the Moon

Die Äpfel rollen unterm Gras,
in Blüten schwelgt das Blut
vor langen Wintern, müde geht
der Trauerzug
hinauf zum Friedhof
zu den Uferlosen
die verkohlt
aus den lachenden Mündern
der Erde schaun.

Die Sonne verdüstert
über dem Weiß des Hügels
den Herbstwind
der durch bleiche Zäune stößt.

Schweigend verwehn auf den Mauern
die Vögel,
in den Stricken der Seele singt
das Fleisch.
Tief unten läßt das Mühlrad
Herz und Hirn erschauern.

Unter dem Eisen des Mondes

The apples roll amid the grass,
blood from long winters
revels in flowers, the funeral procession tires
going up to the cemetery
to those endlessnesses
burned black
that appear from the laughing mouths
of the earth.

Over the white of the hills
the sun darkens
the autumn wind
that blows through white fences.

The birds on the wall silently
drift away,
the flesh
sings in the ropes of the soul.
All the way down the millwheel makes
heart and brain shiver.

Under the Iron of the Moon

Die Erde
tauft meine Kinder.
Schatten stürzen
aus welker Nacht.
Es tropft das Blut der Könige
in die Täler des warmen Brotes.

Die Sterne haben
die Sprache der Lider
die von menschlichen Augen
träumen,
von Hügeln
die von den Messern der Mühsal
zerschnitten sind.

Verflucht sei
diese Qual des Winters
die der Rauch
in heimatlose Wälder treibt
durch die milchigen Ställe der Welt
die der treulose Schlaf erwürgt
an den Ufern unerbittlicher Träume.

Unter dem Eisen des Mondes

The earth
baptizes my children.
Shadows fall
from a pale night.
The blood of kings drips
in valleys of warm bread.

The stars have
that language of eyelids
that dream
of human eyes,
of hills
that are carved up
by knives of misery.

A curse on
this agony of winter
which the smoke
drives into homeless forests
through the milky cowsheds of the world
that this deceitful sleep strangles
on the shores of pitiless dreams.

Under the Iron of the Moon

Meine Kinder kommen,
wenn die Sonne mit einem Seufzer zerfällt,
die Orangen zu sehn
die unter dem Ziegeldach meiner Hütte hängen
und ihre Gesichter klingen lassen wie Glocken.
Wo die Traurigkeit wächst an der Mauer
singt mir die Amsel im Stein
die der Tod geschickt hat von meinen Feldern,
singt
   und singt
im Kern der schweigsamen Julinacht.

Zwischen den Balken stürzen die Möwen
mit wilden Herzen jubelnd ins Meer,
aus den süßen Früchten hör ich die Stimme des Orients
wieder
   im schlechten Schlaf
der mich züchtigt mit dem verlassenen Mond
und dem scharfen Zischen der Schlange.

Unter dem Eisen des Mondes

My children come,
when the sun falls with a sigh,
to see the oranges
hanging from under the roof tiles of my hut,
to make their faces toll like bells.
Where the grief grows on the wall
the blackbird sings to me in the stone
that death sent from my fields,
sings
   and sings
in the hard seed of this silent July night.

Between the rafters the gulls plunge
into the sea crying for joy with their wild hearts,
from the sweet fruit I hear the voice of the Orient
again
   in my bad sleep
that beats me with that deserted moon
and the piercing hiss of the snake.

Under the Iron of the Moon

Ein Schatten meines STERBENS ist das Meer,
die schwarzen Schis stehn im Süden auf
und STERBEN an den Ufern langer Winternächte.

Vergessene Häfen schimmern an den Küsten
des Orients und meine Sprache weht
hinunter an die weißgefalteten Inseln
und höher als die Sterne stehn im Frost
und mit dem Wind der nie mehr kommenden Ruder.

Unwiederbringlich stehn Orangenbäume.
Vergänglich sind die Wellen früher Tage.
Die Schlangen schreiben in den Sand von Mogador
ABSTERBEND ihrer Glieder lange Reise.

Unter dem Eisen des Mondes

That sea is a shadow of my DEATH,
the black ships rising in the south
and PERISHING on the shores of long winter nights.

Forgotten harbors shimmer on the coasts
of the East and my language flutters
down on islands folded in white
and higher than the stars are in the frost
and with that wind of helms no longer coming.

Orange trees stand irretrievable.
The waves of early days can never last.
The snakes are writing in the sands of Mogador
DEADENING the long journey of their limbs.

Under the Iron of the Moon

Die Trauben hängen saftig in die schwarzen
vergessenen Gärten. Müde weht
der Abendwind in diese Zimmer. Seltsam steigt
über den kranken Rücken auf
der runde Mond.

Die Ströme fließen fremd.
Unwirklich blüht in grauer Nacht die Qual.
Des Bruders Leben hebt die roten Lider
zerfallener Städte auf
mit einem Schauer von Erinnerung.

Absterbend weht der Wind über Gitarren
und aufgebrochene Herzen, weht die Nacht
in rote Fenster, tote Spiele,
wo düstere Zeiten sich im Osten nähern.
Unheimlich sind die Schritte ferner Toter
und niederfallende Sterne auf den alten Hügeln
der längst ertrunkenen Stadt.

Unter dem Eisen des Mondes

Grapes hang lush in black
forgotten gardens. The evening wind
blows tiredly into this room. The full moon
rises strangely over
one's suffering back.

The rivers flow differently.
This unreal torment blooms in the gray night.
Your brother's life raises the red eyelids
of fallen cities
with a shiver of memory.

The dying wind blows over guitars
and broken hearts, the night blows
in red windows, dead games,
where dark times draw nearer in the East.
Ominous are the steps of the faraway dead
and falling stars on the ancient hills
of that long-drowned city.

Under the Iron of the Moon

Morgen wird
was war
vertauscht sein
mit dem Himmel
und das Blut der Sonne
niedertropfen
in den Schnee.
Kein Gebet
wird mich am Abend
trösten
und kein Baum
verstehn.

In die Berge
muß mein Kummer ziehn
und die Amsel mich
am frischen Grab
bewachen.

Unter dem Eisen des Mondes

Tomorrow will be
what was
exchanged
for this sky
and the blood of the sun
dripping
in the snow.
No prayer
will console me
this evening
and no tree
will understand.

Into the mountains
my grief must fly
and the blackbird
guard me
in this fresh grave.

Under the Iron of the Moon

Wohin treibt
mich der Wind,
mein Herz,
mein Hirn,
hinunter
in die Stadt,
hinüber
in das Grün
zerwaschener Hügel,
fremden Frauen
   zu
dem Mond,
verschwimmend
weiß
und rot
auf blanker
Kirchhofsmauer,
in den Wald
der schwarz
die Beine streckt
und in den Tümpel
lacht,
aufflattern
wild
im Hieb
vergessene Vögel,
wohin
mein Wind,
mein Herz,
mein Hirn,
mein Weinen?

Unter dem Eisen des Mondes

Where is this wind
taking me,
my heart,
my mind,
going down
into the city,
across
the green
of washed-out hills,
to foreign women
    on
the moon,
blurring together
white
and red
on the shining
churchyard wall,
in this forest
stretching
its black legs
and laughing
in the pond,
flying up
wildly
into this gash
of forgotten birds,
where
my wind,
my heart,
my mind,
my tears?

Under the Iron of the Moon

Hab nicht
meinen Hunger
der
mich frißt
im Winter,
frier nicht
und vergiß den Strauch
der
mir den Mund
mit Laub
und Tränen füllt.

Wart zu Haus
bis ich
zurück bin
im April
und tot
im Bach
die Stimme
meiner Lieder
Wasser trinkt.

Unter dem Eisen des Mondes

Don't partake
of my hunger
that
fed me
in winter,
do not freeze
and forget the thicket
that
fills my mouth
with leaves
and tears.

Wait at home
until I
am back
in April
and dead
in the brook
the voice
of my songs
the water drinks.

Under the Iron of the Moon

Wie der Wind
    läuft er hinunter,
    wie der Wind
in Bäumen hängt sein Messer
    das ein Herz
    aus gelber Sonne schneidet
hinter dem Wald wo seines Frühlings Frau
    blutende Träume flicht,
    grabt ihm nur ein Grab
    und breitet Leinwand aus
    vor seinen blutigen Füßen,
grabt ihm, grabt ihm.

Wie der Wind
    läuft er hinunter,
    wie der Wind
nur Furcht und Trauer trinkend
    die in Träumen
    rollen, feurigem Herbst
    der Todes Pein
    in goldene Schatten wickelt,
düstere Worte in ein Buchenblatt
    im Wind
    läuft er hinunter
    wie der Wind,
einen Stock aus reiner Erde schwingend,
    Himmel schlagend
    daß aus offenen Wunden weißer Wolken
    zitternde Morgen tropfen
in seinen singenden Winter.

Unter dem Eisen des Mondes

Like the wind
   he runs down,
   like the wind
his knife hangs in the trees
   that cut a heart
   from a yellow sun
beyond the forest where the woman of his spring
   weaves bleeding dreams,
   digs a grave just for him
   and spreads out a cloth
   for his bloody feet,
digs for him, digs for him.

Like the wind
   he runs down,
   like the wind
drinking only fear and grief
   that wheel in dreams, in a fiery autumn
   that wraps
   death's anguish
   in golden shadows,
grim words in a beach leaf
   on that wind
   he runs down
   like the wind,
brandishing a stick from the pure earth,
   beating heaven
   so that from the open wounds of white clouds
   mornings drip shivering
in his singing winter.

Under the Iron of the Moon

In den Fischen
und in den Vögeln
ist der Frühling aufgebahrt.

Der Mond spricht mit den Bäumen von des Winters
vergessenen Namen
die in großen Körben faulen
mit zusammengeschrumpftem Gesicht.

Aus schimmernden Krügen trinken wir alle
die Tage der Blüten
die in Grau und Grün gefangen sind
wie ertrunkene Nachtigallen.

Wir trinken und tragen schwarze Gewänder
in unserem eigenen Haus,
denn

in den Fischen
und in den Vögeln
ist der Frühling aufgebahrt.

Unter dem Eisen des Mondes

In the fish,
in the birds
the spring is laid out.

The moon talks to the trees about the winter
of forgotten names
rotting in great baskets
with shriveled faces.

Like drunken nightingales
we all drink days of flowers
caught in gray and green
from shimmering wine cups.

We drink and wear black clothes
in our own house
because

the spring is laid out
in the fish,
in the birds.

Mein Tod kommt bald
über den Acker, müd,
wenn in das Gras
die Schatten stürzen
schwarzer Raben
und hinterm Haus der Baum
die Lider schließt
im Schnee
und nahen Winters
Worte wehn . . .
    Die kranke Seele huscht
umblickend nicht mehr
auf das Dorf,
hinüber.

Unter dem Eisen des Mondes

My death comes soon
across the field, wearily,
as black ravens
cast their shadows
on the grass
as the tree behind the house
shuts its eyes
in the snow
as the words of winter
blow near . . .
     The sick soul no longer darts
looking around
the village,
crossing.

Wenn wir sterbend die milchigen Fenster schließen
    und Feuer machen,
      daß die Stimme des Winters singt
in unserem Fleisch des zerfallenen Sommers
    und ein gutes Wort knistert
      im grünen Ofen,
die Wunde wächst in einem Wald von Tränen,
    die schwarzen Spiegel des Wassers
      und die Ampel des Krieges der vorüber ist,
fürchten wir uns vor dem eiskalten Wind
    und dem beißenden Schnee
      der unsere Gesichter zerreißt
    mit roten Vogeltatzen.

Wenn wir sterbend die milchigen Fenster schließen,
    wird der Frühling
      der uns entging im März,
und der Mittag über dem ländlichen Kirchturm
    der Vögel peinigt und Gras
      und die düstere Trommel schlägt
und Papierwolken flattern läßt als himmlisches Linnen,
    der Frühling zerbrochener Türen,
      zorniger Pfarrer und weißer Blüten,
durch die Flammen des Waldes stoßen mit tausend Zungen
    und unsere Namen unendlichen Namen öffnen
    und stürzen in unser blutendes Herz
das in Schlaf und Trauer schluchzt
    des frühen Herbstes steinigen Preis
    auf verlassenen Totenhügeln.

Unter dem Eisen des Mondes

When we die closing the frosted windows
  and make a fire,
  the voice of winter sings
in our flesh of rotting summer
  and a good word crackles
  in the green stove,
the wound grows in a forest of tears,
  the black mirror of the water
  and the swinging lamp of the war that is over,
we are afraid facing the ice-cold wind
  and the biting snow
  tearing at our faces
  with the red claws of birds.

When we die closing the frosted windows,
  the spring will
  escape us in March,
and above the country church tower noon
  gives pain to the birds and grass
  and beats the grim drum
and makes paper clouds flap like heavenly linen,
  this spring of broken-down doors,
  angry priests, and white flowers
bursting through the burning woods with a thousand tongues
  and opening our names of unending names
  and plunging into our bleeding heart
which sobs in sleep and grief
  the stone price of the early autumn on
  mounds of untended graves.

Under the Iron of the Moon

Die Silben in diesem verregneten März
zerstören das Haus meiner Väter
und wirbeln Schnee in gefalteten Händen auf
und drücken die Augen
einer Verrückten hinter dem Kirchplatz zu.

Die Silben in diesem verregneten März
erheitern ein vergessenes Schaf
und lassen die Milch der Träume
in sieben Dörfern vor den Bergen
die aus Asche sind stocken.

Die Silben in diesem verregneten März
zerfallen über dem Wasser des Flusses
und kehren in langen Nächten zurück
in kranke Gehirne und weiße Tränen,
knisternd über den grünen Gipfeln
einer vertriebenen Frühlingsnacht.

Unter dem Eisen des Mondes

The syllables in this rain-soaked March
batter down the house of my fathers
and stir up the snow in folded hands
and press the eyes shut
of a madman across the church square.

The syllables in this rain-soaked March
cheer up a lost sheep
and let the milk of dreams curdle
in seven villages facing mountains
made of ash.

The syllables in this rain-soaked March
decay over the water of the river
and come back during long nights
in sick brains and white tears,
thundering over the green peaks
of a banished spring night.

Under the Iron of the Moon

Mein Hirn schwimmt am Abend der Sonne zu,
an zerbrochenen Zweigen hängt meine Seele,
in Wäldern treibt mein Frühling, mein Sommer,
müde bin ich wieder, ach, mich schlägt der Stock
der frühen Tage mit Erinnerung.

Mein Hirn schwimmt am Abend der Sonne zu,
trinkend das Blut der Nacht und den Tümpel,
trinkend Hügel, Täler, dumpfe Worte,
schreit im Finstern, schreit vor Stämmen
die in morschen Träumen knarren verrücktes Sterben.

Mein Hirn schwimmt am Abend der Sonne zu,
mein Gott, die Dämmerung schläft, auf kahlen Feldern weht
der Wind, die Wolken treiben
Unruhe in den Tod der mich begräbt
und meines Lachens Blüten schwarzen Vögeln
                in die irren Schnäbel zaubert.

Unter dem Eisen des Mondes

My mind drifts into the evening sun,
my soul hangs in the broken branches,
my spring drifts in the forests, my summer,
I am tired again, oh, the stick of early days
beats me with memory.

My mind drifts into the evening sun,
drinking the blood of night and the pond,
drinking the hills, valleys, dull words,
it cries out in darkness, cries before trees
creaking in rotten dreams from a raving death.

My mind drifts into the evening sun,
my God, the twilight sleeps, the wind blows
across barren fields, the clouds drive
restlessness into this death that buries me
and conjures back my laughter's flowers
   in the wild beaks of black birds.

Under the Iron of the Moon

Im Winter ist alles einfacher,
denn du brauchst keine Welt,
auch nicht das Meer
und niemand wird dich töten.
Es tröstet dich, daß du den Zorn der Tiere
einatmest mit dem Duft der Wälder
die deine Ruh umstehn.
Um Mitternacht wächst Schnee und Eis
und unter schweren Gliedern
schlafen deine Toten.
Du sprichst mit ihnen
wie zur Zeit des Korns
das sie schneiden in Finsternis und Lüge
bis sie der Frühling trinkt
unter der Sonne
die ihren Stachel kranken Rosen raubt.

Unter dem Eisen des Mondes

In winter everything is simpler
because you don't need the world
nor the sea either,
and no one will kill you.
It comforts you as you breathe in the rage
of beasts in the fragrance of the woods
surrounding your peace of mind.
At midnight the snow and ice increase
while under heavy limbs
your dead sleep.
You speak to them
as in those days of grain
which they cut down in darkness and lies
until spring drinks them
under the sun
that steals its sting from sick roses.

Under the Iron of the Moon

Unser Haus trennt die Toten
von Sonne und Mond
und läßt graue Flöten
an kalten Wänden zerspringen
und Lider verlorener Sommer
einfrieren unter dem Kupferdach.
Mit der Amsel stöhnt
der Fluß der Grün und Rot
und Schnee von Tränen scheidet,
schlafende Blumen
von mitternächtlichen Krähenfüßen,
zertretenen Wind
unter Spinngeweben
und das Lachen eines gemästeten Schweines.
Unser Haus zündet giftige Wolken an
und die verbotenen Städte der Angst,
erschlagen liegt
unter der morschen Tür
meines ärmlichen Winters Botschaft.

Unter dem Eisen des Mondes

Our house cuts off the dead
from sun and moon
and lets break
gray pipes on cold walls
and the lost summers's eyelids
freeze under the copper roof.
The river of red and green
moans with the blackbird
and snow distilled from tears,
the sleeping flowers
of midnight crow's feet,
the wind that tramples
through the spider webs
and the laughter of a fattened pig.
Our house ignites poisonous clouds
and the forbidden cities of fear,
killing my humble winter's message
that lies
under the rotten door.

Under the Iron of the Moon

Wie schwer fällt mir ein Wort
an die Verkommenen
die einen Traum nicht unterscheiden können
von den starken Ästen des Birnbaums.

Wie schwer fällt mir ein Wort
auf dieser staubigen Straße
die meinen Schuhen feindlicher ist
als die Sonne dem Schnee
und das Wasser der Wüste.

Wie schwer fällt mir ein Wort
an meinen Vater und an meine Mutter,
wie schwer fällt mir ein Wort
an alle die mich sehen, alternd
in einem erstochenen Herbst.

Wie schwer fällt mir ein Wort
in diesen Tagen die vergeßlich sind.
Wie schwer fällt mir ein Wort.

Unter dem Eisen des Mondes

How hard my word drops
on the depraved
who can't tell a dream
from the strong branches of the pear tree.

How hard my word drops
on this dusty street
unfriendly to my shoes
like sun to snow,
water to the desert.

How hard my word drops
on my father and mother,
how hard my word drops
on everyone watching me, aging
in an autumn stabbed dead.

How hard my word drops
in these days that are oblivious.
How hard my word drops.

Under the Iron of the Moon

Sprich Gras, schrei in den Himmel mein Wort,
von Pflock zu Pflock und über die Wurzeln
springen des Windes rote und gelbe Brüder.

Hör, wie der Strauch brennt und Rauch schießt
durch nasse Mäuler und Fugen,
hör den Schrei der Toten im giftigen Kraut.
Vergiftet sind die Dolden und die Klagen.

Die kranke Mutter sitzt im Stamm und weint
und zählt die Tränen wie im Paradies,
und tausend Schnüre spannt der Wald
von meiner Brust hinauf in das Gesicht der Sonne.

Unter dem Eisen des Mondes

Speak grass, shout my words into the sky,
from stake to stake and over roots
spring the wind's red and yellow brothers.

Listen, as the brush burns and smoke pours
through wet mouths and holes,
hear the dead scream in the poisonous weeds.
Poisoned are the bouquets and the crying.

My sick mother sits in the tree and weeps
and counts her tears as in Paradise,
and a thousand lines stretch through the woods
from my breast to the face of the sun.

Under the Iron of the Moon

Im Namen dessen der auf dem grauen Stein starb
will ich die Vögel nach Süden schicken
wo der Wind durch die schwarzen Wälder weht
Nacht für Nacht und das Mädchen aus dem Brunnen
nichts mehr als Traurigkeit schöpft,
ich will singen in seinem Namen
und Blüten hören in blauen Lüften des Sommers
hinunter blicken in Täler
und Türen und Münder öffnen für den Vergessenen.

Zahl der Vögel, unermeßliche Zahl,
Norden des Meeres,
mein Grab wird seinem gleichen im Weiß der Sprache,
in den Falten des Zorns
und in der Frühe des gefangenen Samens
der zu Staub auf seinen starren Händen wird

im Namen dessen der auf dem grauen Stein starb.

Unter dem Eisen des Mondes

In the name of the one who died on this gray stone,
I want to send the birds south
where wind blows through black woods
night after night and girls draw nothing
from the well but grief,
I want to sing in his name
and hear flowers in the blue air of summer
looking down into valleys,
I want to open doors and mouths for forgetting.

A number of birds, an immeasurable number,
north on the sea,
my grave will be like his in the white of my words,
in the folds of my anger,
and in the dawn of this trapped seed
turning to dust in his frozen hands

in the name of the one who died on this gray stone.

Under the Iron of the Moon

Index of First Lines in German

Index of First Lines in German

Index of First Lines in German

Index of First Lines in English

Index of First Lines in English

Index of First Lines in English

THE LOCKERT LIBRARY OF POETRY IN TRANSLATION

George Seferis: Collected Poems (1924–1955), translated, edited, and introduced by Edmund Keeley and Philip Sherrard

Collected Poems of Lucio Piccolo, translated and edited by Brian Swann and Ruth Feldman

C. P. Cavafy: Selected Poems, translated by Edmund Keeley and Philip Sherrard and edited by George Savidis

Benny Andersen: Selected Poems, translated by Alexander Taylor

Selected Poetry of Andrea Zanzotto, edited and translated by Ruth Feldman and Brian Swann

Poems of René Char, translated and annotated by Mary Ann Caws and Jonathan Griffin

Selected Poems of Tudor Arghezi, translated by Michael Impey and Brian Swann

"The Survivor" and Other Poems, by Tadeusz Różewicz, translated and introduced by Magnus J. Krynski and Robert A. Maguire

"Harsh World" and Other Poems, by Angel González, translated by Donald D. Walsh

Ritsos in Parentheses, translated and introduced by Edmund Keeley

Salamander: Selected Poems of Robert Marteau, translated by Anne Winters

Angelos Sikelianos: Selected Poems, translated and introduced by Edmund Keeley and Philip Sherrard

Dante's "Rime", translated by Patrick S. Diehl

Selected Later Poems of Marie Luise Kaschnitz, translated by Lisel Mueller

Osip Mandelstam's "Stone", translated and introduced by Robert Tracy

The Dawn Is Always New Selected Poetry of Rocco Scotellaro, translated by Ruth Feldman and Brian Swann

Sounds, Feelings, Thoughts: Seventy Poems by Wislawa Szymborska, translated and introduced by Magnus J. Krynski and Robert A. Maguire

The Man I Pretend To Be: "The Colloquies" and Selected Poems of Guido Gozzano, translated and edited by Michael Palma, with an introductory essay by Eugenio Montale

D'Après Tout: Poems by Jean Follain, translated by Heather McHugh

Songs of Something Else: Selected Poems of Gunnar Ekelöf, translated by Leonard Nathan and James Larson

The Little Treasury of One Hundred People, One Poem Each, compiled by Fujiwara No Sadaie and translated by Tom Galt

The Ellipse: Selected Poems of Leonardo Sinisgalli, translated by W. S. Di Piero

The Difficult Days, by Robert Sosa, translated by Jim Lindsey

Hymns and Fragments, by Friedrich Hölderlin, translated and introduced by Richard Sieburth

The Silence Afterwards: Selected Poems of Rolf Jacobson, translated and edited by Roger Greenwald

Rilke: Between Roots, selected poems rendered from the German by Rika Lesser

In the Storm of Roses: Selected Poems by Ingeborg Bachmann, translated, edited, and introduced by Mark Anderson

Birds and Other Relations: Selected Poetry of Dezso Tandori, translated by Bruce Berlind

Brocade River Poems: Selected Works of the Tang Dynasty Courtesan Xue Tao, translated and introduced by Jeanne Larsen

The True Subject: Selected Poems of Faiz Ahmed Faiz, translated by Naomi Lazard

My Name on the Wind: Selected Poems of Diego Valeri, translated by Michael Palma

Aeschylus: The Suppliants, translated by Peter Burian

Foamy Sky: The Major Poems of Miklós Radnóti, selected and translated by Zsuzsanna Ozváth and Frederick Turner

La Fontaine's Bawdy: Of Libertines, Louts, and Lechers, translated by Norman R. Shapiro

A Child Is Not a Knife: Selected Poems of Göran Sonnevi, translated and edited by Rika Lesser

George Seferis: Collected Poems, Revised Edition, translated, edited, and introduced by Edmund Keeley and Philip Sherrard

C. P. Cavafy: Collected Poems, Revised Edition, translated and introduced by Edmund Keeley and Philip Sherrard and edited by George Savidis

Selected Poems of Shmuel HaNagid, translated from the Hebrew by Peter Cole

The Late Poems of Meng Chiao, translated by David Hinton

Leopardi: Selected Poems, translated by Eamon Gennan

Through Naked Branches: Selected Poems of Tarjei Vesaas, translated and edited by Roger Greenwald

The Complete Odes and Satires of Horace, translated with introduction and notes by Sidney Alexander

Selected Poems of Solomon Ibn Gabirol, translated by Peter Cole

Puerilities: Erotic Epigrams of The Greek Anthology, translated by Daryl Hine

Night Journey, by María Negroni, tr by Anne Twitty

The Poetess Counts to 100 and Bows Out, by Ana Enriqueta Terán, translated by Marcel Smith

Nothing Is Lost: Selected Poems by Edward Kocbek, translated by Michael Scammell and Veno Taufer, and introduced by Michael Scammell

The Complete Elegies of Sextus Propertius, translated with introduction and notes by Vincent Katz

Knowing the East, by Paul Claudel, translated with introduction and notes by James Lawler

Enough to Say It's Far: Selected Poems of Pak Chaesam, by Pak Chaesam, translated by David R. McCann and Jiwon Shin

In Hora Mortis/Under the Iron of the Moon: Poems, by Thomas Bernhard, translated by James Reidel